BERLITZ®

BRITTANY

1989/1990 Edition

By the staff of Berlitz Guides
A Macmillan Company

Berlitz Trademark Reg. U.S. Patent Office and other countries –
Marca Registrada. Library of Congress Catalog Card No. 84-73296.

Printed in Switzerland by Weber S.A., Bienne.

4th Printing
1989/1990 Edition

How to use our guide

- All the **practical information**, hints and tips that you will need before and during the trip start on p. 104.
- For **general background**, see the sections Brittany and the Bretons, p. 6, and A Brief History, p. 12.
- All the principal **sights** to visit are discussed between pp. 24 and 87.
  - 🚶 Our own choice of sights most highly recommended is pin-pointed by the Berlitz traveller symbol.
- **Sports** and **leisure activities** are described between pp. 87 and 90.
- A rundown of suggestions of **purchases** to look out for is on p. 91.
- **Entertainment, Folklore, Festivals** and **Events** in general figure between pp. 92 and 96.
- Finally, the pleasures and possibilities of **eating out** in Brittany are covered between pp. 97 and 103.
- The **index** on p. 127 gives place names occurring in the guide.

Although we make every effort to ensure the accuracy of all the information in this book, changes occur incessantly. We cannot therefore take responsibility for facts, prices, addresses and circumstances in general that are constantly subject to alteration. Our guides are updated on a regular basis as we reprint, and we are always grateful to readers who let us know of any errors, changes or serious omissions they come across.

Text: Giles Allen
Photography: Claude Huber
Layout: Doris Haldemann
We would like to thank Gérard Chaillon, Henri Séité and Yvon Bonnot for their help with the preparation of this guide. Furthermore we are very grateful to the tourist offices of Brittany, the Syndicats d'Initiative, and to the Délégation régionale du Tourisme, Rennes, for their cooperation.
Ⓕ Cartography: Falk-Verlag, Hamburg.

Cover photo: Bénodet

pp. 2–3: Côte Sauvage, Quiberon peninsula

Contents

Brittany and the Bretons

Pounded by mighty waves or lapped by gentle ripples, the coastline gives Brittany its character. Surrounded on three sides by the sea, Brittany is a kind of island, sheltered and self-contained yet extraordinarily open to the outside world. Contradictory? For sure. Remote? Sometimes. Inhospitable? Anything but.

Almost as big as Belgium, but with only a quarter of its population (roughly 3 million inhabitants), Brittany is the Far West of Europe. Not for nothing was the Continent's furthermost point called *finis terrae* (land's end). Countless millennia ago the province was a kind of western alpine region, with

Light and lacy: the arch of Le Folgoët and local coiffe.

mountains sheering up from the sea; but the elements eroded the peaks to a series of bumps and dales. Today other Frenchmen jeer at Brittany's "summit" in the Monts d'Arrée, a mere 1,260 feet high, until they hike up and gaze in awe at the breathtaking desolation and natural beauty before them.

With a coastline over 750 miles long, Brittany obviously lives in very close contact with the sea, that has forged the land as it has forged the people. No point is more than 50 miles from the Atlantic or the English Channel, which meet midway around the coast. Made up of four *départements**, the Ille-et-Vilaine, the Côtes-du-Nord, Finistère and Morbihan, Brittany divides topographically into two parts, Haute-Bretagne or Upper Brittany (in fact the low-lying eastern area) and Basse-

---

* Loire Atlantique, with its capital at Nantes, was removed administratively speaking from the Breton region.

Bretagne or Lower Brittany, the hilly western region. The first is mostly inland, while Basse-Bretagne occupies the greater part of the coast.

However you approach Brittany, from the gentle Loire Valley, lush Normandy or the Maine, the fertile heartland of France, you know that there is something different about it, something specifically Breton. It's partly a style of architecture: cantilevered, wood-panelled medieval houses and weather-beaten granite structures alternate with modern villas. Sparklingly clean and dazzlingly white, the latter have dark-grey slate roofs and green or brown shutters. It's partly, too, the landscape: compared with neighbouring provinces, it is harsh, rugged, tormented. Windswept moors, the *lande,* covered with heather, broom, fern and bracken, merge into neat enclosed fields and meadows. Limpid streams and rivers ripple secretively through gorse-filled prairies. Black cows dot the hills and dales. Ragged, jagged coastlines give way suddenly to smooth, sandy beaches.

Most of all, however, Brittany owes its unique character to the people, the Bretons. To outsiders they seem eminently French, with the same reactions, the same gestures and ways of thought. And they are. But Frenchmen from elsewhere often see them as a breed apart.

Although all Bretons speak French, many (around a million) converse in Breton at home. The language is taught at school, and committees defend Breton culture and traditions with ardour. The Bretons, whether French-speaking or Breton-speaking, are not as exuberant as the inhabitants of southern France, nor are they as closed as their countrymen in the north. Their propensity for story-telling, their superstition, their deeply held religious feelings all bring them nearer the Irish and the Welsh than anybody.

If Bretons are so different, history provides an easy explanation. *Armorica,* Brittany's Roman name, had barely been colonized by the Romans, along with the rest of Gaul, when waves of settlers from Great Britain, fleeing the Angle and Saxon invasions, populated the land. This time the Celtic language came to stay. The Breton nation was formed

The picturesque Channel port of Roscoff lives from the sea.

8

and its customs developed. The region received its Breton name, *Breizh* (meaning Britain), while Gaul, the rest of France-to-be, went its Latin way.

Brittany has been officially linked to France since 1532, but relations have blown hot and cold. The province long supplied France with human cannon fodder. It served as a larder for Paris and provided the capital with servants. In the last century, Brittany was the butt of jokes about backwardness.

Brittany's principal role in French history has, naturally enough, been maritime. From here, from the great ports of Saint-Malo, Brest and Lorient, came a high proportion of the country's sailors—and pirates. Even today, Brittany remains the cradle of the French navy.

If the number of fishermen decreases as their profit margins dwindle, and if they have to venture further and further afield as the fishing banks are depleted, the colourful fleets of trawlers still provide a note of gaiety in the harbours. And the night-time *criée,* when the tunny fish, lobster and crab are unloaded and auctioned off, remains a fascinating spectacle. Fishing and agriculture, in spite of the increase in industry, remain the cornerstones of Breton activities.

Brittany comes second only to the French Riviera in the holiday popularity stakes, but there's been no large-scale urbanization of the coast here. The climate, much maligned, is surprisingly clement—especially in the Morbihan region of southern Brittany—although there are plenty of mild microclimates in the north round Dinard and Roscoff and on the island of Bréhat. It's medically recognized that a holiday beside the sea in Brittany is a tonic for the depressed and tired. Moreover, Brittany is the centre in France of thalassotherapy (sea-water therapy), an alternative treatment for all sorts of ailments.

North Brittany's best clean sandy beaches with gentle slopes down to the water are at Dinard on the Emerald Coast and at Perros-Guirec on the "Pink" Granite Coast. In the south, where the sea may be a degree or so warmer, there are superb beaches at Bénodet or Beg-Meil in Finistère, at Quiberon, Carnac and, most glorious of all, La Baule. A beach barely big enough to hold a few bathers in the morning becomes at low tide a vast expanse of clear golden sand. The effect of the tide means the scene is never static, but always on the move, as the sea fills with swimmers, sailors, windsurfers and divers, while the beaches come to life with volleyball players, with clubs of young people doing gymnastics, with fishermen or shellfish searchers.

Few resist the temptation to try and catch their evening meal. Nowhere in the whole of France can you find such fantastic seafood. Most desirable, biggest and most difficult to find is the *tourteau,* a kind of crab. You might need a bent wire to coax this creature out of a hole. There are also cockles, periwinkles, crabs and a multitude of other shellfish to be found in the puddles and pools left by the receding tide. Follow the crowds to the best spots.

But if it's in the realm of beach activities that Brittany excels, never forget that inland there's plenty more to do as well. You can hike across the Monts d'Arrée or cycle over lanes and little-frequented paths. Drift along the rivers Aulne or Odet, or take a barge down the canals that crisscross the countryside. If you want to get away from people, there's no problem. If, however, you want to do some sightseeing, there's plenty enough to keep you busy for days on end.

The cities of Rennes and Nantes (Brittany's only real metropolis) have fascinating old centres, as have smaller towns such as Morlaix, Vannes, Quimper, Dinan and Tréguier. The fortified walled cities of Concarneau, Saint-Malo and Guérande are marvels by any standards. Castles like the warlike Fougères and fairytale Vitré contrast with such Renaissance or part-Renaissance fortresses as Josselin or Kerjean. Cathedral-lovers have a choice between Dol, Quimper or Tréguier, among a whole variety of others. As to churches, abbeys, monasteries and chapels, calvaries and parish closes, Brittany is so liberally endowed that it is hard to single out any favourites.

Dawn and dusk are the best times to contemplate Brittany's megaliths. Swathed in mist, their mystery, majesty and intriguing beauty impress all who behold them. The major sites at Carnac obviously take pride of place, but Brittany is scattered with such objects, some modern hoaxes, some stranded in the middle of fields and used by farmers as gateposts.

Brittany's charm lies in a subtle mix between nature and the man-made, hamlets and villages, heathland and farms, perfectly preserved medieval town centres, superb visions of the sea. Mists swirl around **11** ghostly tree trunks. The wind-swept moors break into gold and purple as the broom and heather come to life. Church towers and steeples, fine as lace, peek over the brows of hills. The fishing ports lie under leaden skies, draped in a faint air of tragedy, fleets of brightly painted fishing boats bobbing in harbours chock-a-block with sailing boats and pleasure craft. Views and poetry, intimately mixed—that's what Brittany is all about.

A Brief History

The history of Brittany began long before the Bretons arrived on the misty prow of Europe, and indeed long before the Celts reached the shores of present-day France. At about the time the ancient Egyptians were erecting the pyramids, between 5500 and 3500 B.C., a mysterious people were putting up mighty rows of stones at Carnac and other spots in Brittany. They transported the

huge boulders over considerable distances, arranging them in an order that must have had social or religious connotations. Their precise function still baffles, but the majestic effect of these rows of stones, doubtless erected in stages over many centuries, cannot fail to impress even today. They are the last vestiges of a civilization that vanished. Only Stonehenge in Britain has quite the same evocative appeal.

The fate of Brittany's earliest inhabitants is not known. The Celts or Gauls (as those who settled in France came to be known) probably annihilated or absorbed them when they rolled into Brittany from the East in waves between the 6th and 4th centuries B.C. The Gauls apparently left the great stones as they were, adapting them to their own Druidic purposes. Then, as up till recently, Brittany must have been isolated: sea on three sides, a thick curtain of forest on the fourth. The Gauls called it *Armor* (Land by the Sea).

Romanization

A collection of quarrelsome Celtic tribes, the Gauls had been settled into the whole of France including Brittany for some centuries when the invincible well-oiled machine of the Roman army steamrollered through the country under Caesar in 56 B.C., meeting resistance all the way. When he reached Armorica, five distinct tribes occupied the region. Caesar describes how his boats, well armed but cumbersome, defeated the Veneti (that had settled around Vannes)—thanks to a drop in the wind.

As night falls, the gesticulating world of the calvary comes to life. 13

The Romans colonized the far-away province of Armorica, even though it appears guerilla bands made life hard for them. A popular French comic strip titled *Astérix* gives an idea of the epic struggle between Romans and Gauls. Truth to tell, the Romans easily won the day. They went on to construct roads and villas and established an administrative infrastructure. Brittany slipped out of sight for a while until the barbarian invasions brought about a complete eclipse in the 5th century A.D.

At about the same time, in nearby Britain, invasions by Angles, Jutes and Saxons were driving back the island Celts (the Britons, cousins of the Gauls in France). Over the next two centuries, their religious leaders led them into exile to Brittany. They brought with them their religion, Christianity, and reinstated their language, transferring many of the place names of their former homeland. They transplanted their legends to Brittany, too. Thus King Arthur and his Knights of the Round Table, Lancelot of the Lake, Tristan and Iseult, Merlin and Morgan are just as at home in Brittany as in their original setting. You will meet them everywhere, particularly in the interior.

Brittany Takes Shape

A certain anarchy reigned for years, and there must have been frequent skirmishes with the Franks on the marches. Charlemagne rose to power, subduing Brittany in 799. Under the Carolingian crown, the province remained a loose grouping of semi-autonomous parishes. Then, in 826, the French Emperor, Louis the Pious, appointed a Breton nobleman from Vannes, a certain Nominoë, to oversee the province, raising him to the rank of duke. For 20-odd years, Nominoë administered faithfully for his Frankish overlords, bringing law and order to the province. In 845, after Louis' death, he threw off the yoke of Frankish obedience which bound him to Louis and defeated his successor, King Charles the Bald, at Ballon near Redon. Nominoë, self-styled king of Brittany, extended his domain virtually to the limits of the present-day province of Brittany (plus Nantes). The kingdom he and his son Erispoë forged survived intact for nearly a century.

Early in the 10th century,

Five thousand years on, Brittany's megalithic monuments still stand erect against the elements.

the Normans wrought havoc throughout Brittany. Dire poverty and suffering were the lot of the Bretons whose leaders fled to Britain, their former homeland. Alain Barbe-Torte, a nobleman's son, returned from exile in England to deliver the Normans a sound defeat in 939, but, nevertheless, Brittany remained isolated and disordered, while neighbouring France unified and grew ever more powerful.

At this point, two major wars rearranged the game. Hostilities between England and France broke out, and the interminable Hundred Years' War (1337-1453) began. In Brittany itself, Duke Jean III the Good died (1341), leaving no direct successor. The War of Succession pitted his niece, Jeanne de Penthièvre, against his half-brother, Jean I de Montfort. Inevitably the "superpowers", France and England, got involved, each choosing a protégé: the French backed Jeanne de Penthièvre (whose husband, Charles de Blois, was a nephew of the French King, Philippe VI), the English, Jean I de Montfort.

Brittany's Golden Age

Finally, in 1364, at the Battle of Auray, Jean II de Montfort emerged victorious and Charles de Blois met his end. After the Treaty of Guérande, Brittany was able to lick its wounds. The dukes of Montfort, particularly the victor (who became Jean IV) and his successor Jean V, observed a position of strict, prudent (and profitable) neutrality towards France and England, launching an unprecedented spate of construction and business activity. Agriculture improved and the Breton fleet grew in size and strength. Brittany's major châteaux date from this time.

But prosperity bred envy, and the French looked on greedily as Breton wealth increased. After skirmishes with Louis XI of France, Duke François II, trying to hold back French encroachment, was decisively beaten at Saint-Aubin-du-Cormier on July 28, 1488. He was forced to sign the Treaty of Verger, abrogating certain Breton prerogatives. He died, it's said, of a broken heart, that same year.

In order to hold the French at a distance, his daughter, Duchess Anne, who was 12 at the time, married the German king Maximilian of Austria, by proxy in 1490. When the French again invaded, she was forced to "divorce" and marry Charles VIII of France. The starving people of Rennes, be-

Sturdy medieval Josselin sports an elaborate Renaissance façade.

sieged by the French army, begged Anne to meet Charles. And in a rare historical "happily-ever-after" situation, the two took an immediate fancy to each other and fell in love outside the walls of Rennes. Anne became Queen of France in 1491, while remaining duchess of Brittany; she skilfully managed to keep Brittany independent, linked to France but with a separate administration.

Eight years later Charles died in an accident, aged 28, without any offspring; within a year Anne married the successor to the throne, Louis XII, who repudiated his wife for her. Again French kingdom and Breton duchy were kept separate, but the end of autonomy for Brittany was drawing nigh. Anne died in 1514, and her daughter Claude married the Duke of Angoulême, who was to become François I of France. The duchy was ceded by Claude to the crown in 1532; in Vannes the Breton Parliament ratified the Treaty of Perpetual Union with France. From now on, Breton history largely parallels that of France. **17**

From Independence to Gloire

Union initially meant confidence, and a surge of pride and activity. Voyages of exploration took Bretons far afield (Jacques Cartier from Saint-Malo explored the St. Lawrence Estuary in 1534), and the province's maritime ports put it in good stead to trade with the Americas. Manors, castles and churches galore went up, designed in a new style for a new age—that of the Renaissance. France, under François I, prospered.

But serious religious divisions brought new conflict; France was split between Protestants (Huguenots) and Catholics, and dissension inevitably reached largely Catholic Brittany. Taking advantage of the situation, the governor of the province, the Duke of Mercœur, revolted in 1588. He declared himself head of the Catholic League and, with the help of Spain, attempted to reclaim Breton independence (for his own benefit). A civil war broke out, and bands of outlaws terrorized the countryside, till the Bretons finally begged Henri IV, who had forsworn Protestantism in 1591, to come to the rescue. Henri complied, signing the famous Edict of Nantes (1598), granting religious freedom and tolerance to all.

Brittany Rules the Waves

The glory that France acquired over the next centuries under Louis XIV, *Roi Soleil,* and his successors shone on Brittany, too. Nantes prospered from its triangular trade in African slaves and Antilles rum, sugar and spices. Lorient, home port of the French East India Company, reached its apogee around 1750; Brest became France's chief naval port; Saint-Malo flourished as a base for privateers.

But glory and absolute monarchy—symbolized by the splendid monuments and fine buildings that went up in Nantes and Rennes—were achieved at the expense of the impoverished Breton peasantry. Their simmering resentment exploded into open revolt in 1675 when a law was introduced, requiring all official documents to be recorded on special stamped paper—entailing additional taxation. The uprising began in the main towns, with the sacking of tax offices and treasuries. It spread throughout the province and sparked off other insurrections (such as that of the famous Bonnets rouges), before it was savagely put down by royal French troops.

Smaller uprisings against the central government occurred periodically, until the Parliament of Brittany and its public prosecutor, La Chalotais, collided with the governor, d'Aiguillon, in 1764—again on the subject of taxes. For several years, Brittany's Parliament remained in a state of rebellion against the king and central authority. Something was astir: the first murmurings of the French Revolution.

Backslide

Given the general neglect with which the isolated and poor province was treated by successive kings, it was hardly surprising that Brittany welcomed the Revolution in 1789 with open arms. Yet the brutal excesses and the mass drownings in Nantes disgusted the Bretons; attacks against the Church and mass levies for the Napoleonic campaigns—expressly forbidden in the Treaty of Perpetual Union with France—further dampened their enthusiasm for the new order. Thus, within a few years, the fervent Breton revolutionary became an equally fervent *Chouan,* or royalist. For a few years things calmed down. Then under Georges Cadoudal resentment against

Going, going, gone: fish up for auction at the morning criée.

Bonaparte flared up again. Damage was inflicted on the Napoleonic army, but Cadoudal was caught and executed in 1804 and the revolt was at an end.

The centralizing force of the Napoleonic system isolated Brittany more and more. During the 19th century, attempts were made to stamp out the Breton language—which was considered demeaning—and church sermons were no longer delivered in the vernacular. Even the advent of the railway failed to bring development, but served rather to draw large numbers of Bretons to settle in Paris. Brittany was considered something of a backwater.

World War I found the province in a piteous state, but with plentiful manpower to supply the trenches. Although the fighting took place on distant battlefields of France, no less than one Breton soldier in four was killed in the butchery, or some 240,000 in all. In spite of this sacrifice, consideration for Brittany and its general situation barely improved after the war. Local indignation reached new heights in 1925, when a law was enacted against the Breton language. From this time date the first calls for independence, and the beginning of the autonomy movement.

Take-Off

During World War II, after the fall of France, the Germans were not slow to take advantage of latent nationalist feelings. This later gave rise to a regrettable settling of scores, in which sincere Breton nationalists found themselves equated with collaborators. However, Brittany more than played its part in the Resistance. Just after General de Gaulle's famous radio broadcast on June 18, 1940, urging the French to fight on, the islanders of Sein—to a man—left their wives and children to rally to the Free French in London. Brittany's ports and naval installations suffered severe bombardments, and the town centres of Brest, Saint-Malo, Lorient and Saint-Nazaire had to be rebuilt.

After the war, Brittany began to develop as never before. Several different factors were responsible: the tourist boom, a new awareness in Paris of the area's needs and aspirations, help in financing big projects, the modernization of agriculture and a policy of decentralization that encouraged new industries such as telecommunications to relocate in Brittany. Gradually a new Brittany began to emerge—a modern Brittany, no longer isolated, fully up with the latest techniques, creative, dynamic, innovative.

Two disastrous oil spills that sullied Brittany's coasts in 1967 and 1978 are events of the past. Although not untouched by recession or the world economic crisis, Brittany is weathering the storm as well as any part of France. And the new recognition accorded to the Breton language, accompanied by a return to Celtic roots, has given the province more self-respect than it has enjoyed since its days as a dukedom.

Sun, sea—and solitude. Two's company on this Breton beach.

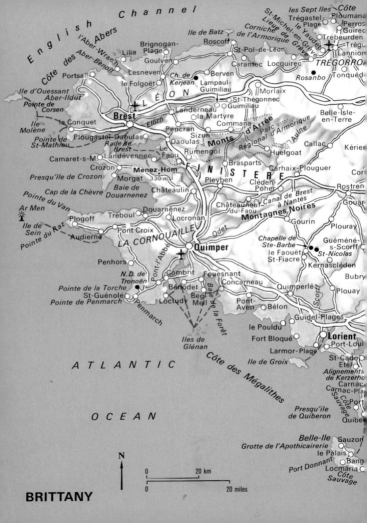

BRITTANY

Where to Go

With over 750 miles of coast-line—and a sinuous, serrated coastline at that—Brittany can be rather difficult to get around. Although dual carriageways (divided highways) do, in fact, circle much of the province, making travel between the larger towns relatively simple, it's not at all easy to go from one coastal area to another. Because of Brittany's sheer size we have had to limit the sights visited, hence a cruel but compulsory choice, of necessity arbitrary on occasions.

We have chosen to start on the north coast with Saint-Malo, one of the most important points of entry to Brittany. From there we continue, with excursions off to convenient points (such as the unforgettable Mont-Saint-Michel) mostly counter-clockwise to "land's end", the Pointe du Raz, and on along the south coast to La Baule, finishing with the interior and the eastern areas bordering "France". Of course, all sorts of variations are possible; within easy reach of all the coastal regions are delightful sights inland.

Farmland and meadows dictate
24 *the feel of Brittany's interior.*

Saint-Malo and the Côte d'Emeraude

A jewel of a town, Saint-Malo holds the key to the Emerald Coast, so called for the range of hues of the sea, from green to indigo. From Saint-Malo to Le Val-André, a string of ports, beaches and resorts sweeps west for some 40 miles.

Saint-Malo Area

The whole history of **Saint-Malo** is one of fierce pride, pride in achievement, in independence and in maritime traditions. St. Malo, a Welsh saint, settled in the 6th century on what was—at least at high tide—an island. Although the fortified *ville intra-muros* spilled over the walls to become a teeming city of nearly 50,000, the core, the old city, lives in proud isolation, surrounded on three sides by the open sea and port. Flattened by air raids and bombardments during the last war, Saint-Malo rose from its ashes, in similar form to before—one of the most successful of recent restorations.

In the high season, group tours of the **ramparts** run every hour and are well worth taking. The walls, built in the 12th century and altered over and over again until the 18th, command superb vistas out over the sea, the beaches and, inwards, over the town itself.

Between Saint-Philippe bastion and Tour Bidouane, the whole Emerald Coast opens up: the Rance Estuary, with, way in the distance, Cap Fréhel, and somewhat nearer, Dinard beach. In front lie the islets of Grand-Bé, Petit-Bé and Cézembre: at low tide you can walk or wade to Grand-Bé for the views out over the ocean and to visit the simple tomb

of François-René de Chateaubriand, the Romantic writer, who chose to be buried here. Don't forget to return as soon as the tide turns—or you may find yourself trapped!

A popular attraction lies just below the steps beside Porte Saint-Thomas: the **Aquarium,** where fauna from the seas all around frolic in tanks built right into the ramparts.

The tower of **Quic-en-Groigne** houses an interesting **waxworks museum,** recounting the history of Saint-Malo and bringing vividly to life the colourful swashbuckling characters of times past. More relics and reminders of old Saint-Malo are on view in the **Musée d'Histoire de la Ville,** just across Place Chateaubriand. Exhibits, mostly with a seafaring angle, include everything

Serene within its ramparts, Saint-Malo defies time and tides.

from sailors' trunks to colossal ships' figureheads.

Place Chateaubriand, brimming over with hotels and cafés, is a good place to take a break. From here head on into the centre through a delightful maze of streets to the **Cathédrale Saint-Vincent**, begun in the 12th century and heavily restored after the last war. The openwork tower rising way above the walls is visible from far and wide. Inside light streams through modern stained-glass windows.

No tour of Saint-Malo is really complete without a visit to the neighbouring resort of **Saint-Servan-sur-Mer** (a suburb of Greater Saint-Malo), reached through a distinctly uncharming port area. Make a stop at the exceptionally interesting **Musée International du Long-Cours Cap-Hornier** in Tour Solidor. Displays vividly recreate life aboard the old Cape Horn sailing vessels, illustrating techniques, traditions and the daily life of sailors who negotiated the rough Cape waters.

A walk round the **Corniche d'Aleth** will help you get your bearings and allow you to appreciate from afar the perfect proportions of Saint-Malo, ringed by golden beaches, with islands beyond, and the messy dockland area behind.

The coast road east to Cancale (23 km.), skirting **Paramé** reaches **Pointe du Grouin**: advance to the tip of this rocky outcrop, 145 feet above the sea. On a stormy day the effects can be most powerful. The view encompasses the craggy bird sanctuary of Ile des Landes, the distant Norman town of Granville and Cap Fréhel—an impressive span.

Cancale means oysters, oysters galore, oysters sold individually *(au détail)* or in great baskets *(bourriches)*. Follow your nose down to the stalls on the beach; all around, oyster beds stretch off into the muddy distance. Cancale is also a pretty port, with small fishermen's houses skirting the harbour. The main square has a profusion of restaurants—oyster and fish restaurants, naturally.

The long Bay of Mont-Saint-Michel swoops round towards the superb Abbey of Mont-Saint-Michel on its mountain-top, which grows steadily bigger and more inspiring as you approach. Technically, it's just in Normandy, but don't miss a chance to visit.

As impressive from near as far, the Abbey of Mont-Saint-Michel stands one step closer to heaven.

The Mont-Saint-Michel

Often called "Wonder of the Western World", the abbey-fortress remains long in the memory, for its setting atop a rocky hill with a vast sandy bay all around, for its incomparably fine architecture, for its history and the sheer magnitude of the achievement.

It all started in the 8th century, when Aubert, Bishop of Avranches, had a vision in which the Archangel Michael commanded him to build an oratory on the island of Tombe. Soon pilgrims were drawn to the place and new buildings had to be put up. Fired by a spirit of faith, Bene-

dictine monks set about the task, and in 1017 work on the abbey proper began. Raised on a platform nearly 250 feet above sea level, building spurted ahead early in the 13th century with the construction of the almonry, Knights' Hall, refectory and cloisters, known collectively as the Marvel *(la Merveille)*. Defences were put up, mostly in the 14th century, followed by a grandiose Flamboyant Gothic replacement for the chancel of the church, which collapsed in 1421.

Most visitors approach the Mont via the half-mile-long causeway constructed in 1874. But the pilgrims of old made their way here at low tide, traversing the treacherous quicksands left by the receding sea. Today threatened by a silting up of the bay, Mont-Saint-Michel is an island only during moon tides when the sea rises at a rate of nearly 50 yards a minute, covering a distance of ten miles or so. Prudence is the order of the day for those who wish to follow the pilgrims' route: fogs can come up all of a sudden, and it's easy to lose your bearings.

To visit the abbey, you have to join one of the multilingual guided tours, which take just under an hour. As you wander **30** up and down through a confus-

ing progression of rooms, remember that the abbey complex occupies three distinct levels, situated one on top of another: the *lower,* with storeroom and almonry; the *middle,* site of the Knights' Hall and Guest Hall; and the *upper,* given over to the church, cloister and refectory.

The visit starts from the terrace on top, with superb views of the bay and church façade, and works downwards. The **abbey church** offers striking contrasts between the rugged simplicity of the Romanesque nave and the elegant dynamism of the Flamboyant Gothic chancel, while the **cloister,** with its delicate columns and tiny garden, is a sheer marvel of lightness and grace.

The **refectory** has perfect acoustics, which enabled every monk to follow the lessons that were read amid the clatter of cutlery. Note, too, its unique lighting system. No less impressive are the **Crypte des Gros-Piliers,** with its ten massive pillars, and the **Knights' Hall** *(Salle des Chevaliers),* one of the finest Gothic halls in the world.

Surly seas are for the birds. Boatman (below) has clear sailing.

West from Saint-Malo

Fashionable **Dinard** has enjoyed over a century of glory since its "discovery" by Anglo-American travellers in the 1850s. A broad sheltered beach, one of the best in northern Brittany, a particularly mild micro-climate—palm, fig trees, tamarisk and camellias flourish here—and easy access across the Channel make it an obvious favourite. Dinard has all the elements of the perfect resort: luxury villas, long paved promenades, plush hotels, smart shops, a "serious" casino, parks and gardens, discotheques and an Olympic public swimming pool. A faintly Victorian atmosphere persists, adding to Dinard's appeal.

Nearby **Saint-Lunaire** has plenty of old-fashioned charm, too. Its busy main beach stretches away towards the Pointe du Décollé. A stroll here is the "constitutional" that most visitors take for some of the coast's best views up (to Cap Fréhel) and down (to Saint-Malo).

Saint-Briac-sur-Mer, further along, smacks of a neat and cheerful family resort with plenty of activities from golf and riding to deep-sea fishing expeditions, while **Lancieux,** another quiet family resort, offers a sensible beach, sailing school, fishing, tennis and mini-golf. Several miles on you come to **Saint-Jacut-de-la-Mer,** situated at the centre of a tapering peninsula jutting out between two sizable bays. Fishermens' paradise, and bathers', too, the resort tends to get very full in summer.

Continue on the main road through LE GUILDO, notable for the ruins of a legendary castle, to **Saint-Cast,** one of the north coast's high points, with its sweeping beach hedged in by Pointe de la Garde and Pointe de Saint-Cast. In 1758, during the course of the Seven Years' War, the English and Welsh suffered a humiliating defeat

Fort-La-Latte lives up to everyone's idea of a sturdy feudal castle.

here at the hands of the Duc d'Aiguillon, losing 2,400 men.

Next stop lies across the gaping Baie de la Frênaye: **Fort-la-Latte,** considered one of the most romantic castles in Brittany for its setting beside the sea. A ten-minute trek on foot through shrub and flower, past a creditable **menhir,** the Doigt de Gargantua, leads to the château of red stone. Perched on a rocky spur and attached to the mainland by two drawbridges with the sea gurgling below, Fort-la-Latte has seen many a

drama enacted within its precincts. Though the fort was much altered over the centuries, the *donjon,* a "chesspiece" keep atop a knoll, dates intact from the 13th and 14th centuries. The watchtower, above a slippery stepped roof, affords a panoramic view of the coastline. With a guide you will visit the inner court, the guardroom, governor's residence, and chapel, not forgetting the cannon ball smeltery, equipped with an apparatus for cooling the cannon balls when 33 they emerged red hot—and an infamous trap-door over the sea.

Cap Fréhel offers one of the great moments of a visit to Brittany. From cliffs 237 feet above the raging seas, you survey a stirring spectacle: a wild, open promontory, treeless and windswept, a chaos of reddish sandstone and black schist, and the tortured rocks of the Grande and Petite Fauconnière bird sanctuaries, scattered with colonies of cormorants and black guillemots. Ascend the new (1950) square lighthouse and you can take in a sweep of 70 miles on a good day.

Sables-d'Or-les-Pins, a nearby seaside resort complete with casino, amid golden sand dunes and pine forest, offers a change of scenery and a change of pace. Neighbouring **Erquy** is a charming family resort, developing in all directions. To the west campers cling like cockles to the shoreline, while to the east restaurants and shops fringe the bay. Down at the port, trawlers unload crates of fish and, in particular, Erquy's speciality: unbeatable scallops *(coquilles Saint-Jacques).* A few miles beyond, cosy **Le Val-André** provides the pleasures of Erquy on a more intimate scale. A pleasant promenade fronts the beach.

Inland

Historic castles, towns and sights are sprinkled through the gentle, but hilly countryside, within a few miles of the coast. To mention but a few: **Lamballe,** a quiet *bourg* with a national stud-farm; **Moncontour,** a "perfect" medieval village, perched like an eagle's nest at 550 feet; the evocative ruins of **La Hunaudaye,** a 13th-17th-century castle.

But medieval Brittany seems most alive, most real, most close in **Dinan.** Behind stone ramparts, the old centre of town vibrates with life. The sagging, cantilevered, wood-fronted dwellings, leaning crazily on each other, today house butchers shops, pharmacies and bakers. Thus Dinan prospers, as it has for centuries past, full of flowers and charm, with a maze of tiny streets.

The town lies at the head of the Rance Estuary, on a rocky spur towering above the river. By the time William the Conqueror besieged Dinan in 1065, the original Roman fort had become a fortified city with a castle. It figures as such on the famous Bayeux Tapestry.

Pay a visit to the **museum** in the Tour de Coëtquen, situated in the 1382 castle. The collection includes splendid examples of Breton furniture and costumes. The tourist office occupies the 16th-century **Hôtel Kératry,** a fine old house in the Rue de l'Horloge. Next door, the Tour de l'Horloge, a quadrangular tower dating from the end of the 15th century, stresses the close connections between Anne de Bretagne and Dinan: in 1507 she donated one of the four bronze bells in the belfry.

Charming streets thread through the town. This is the sort of place you meander in, particularly around **Place des Merciers** and **Place des Cordeliers.** The most characteristic thoroughfares, **Rue du Jerzual** and **Rue du Petit Fort** connect up and lead down to the **port,** winding between two perfect rows of restored and protected artisans' houses.

Dol-de-Bretagne is a sleepy inland town. Yet in the 12th century, not only was Dol beside the sea, but it resounded with all the activity and bustle of a capital. In the intervening years, the marshland was reclaimed from the sea, and history somehow forgot it.

Nominoë was crowned Duke of Brittany in Dol in 848. The town paid a heavy tribute during the wars with Normandy, but worse was to come with King John of England, who burned the cathedral in 1203. Stricken with remorse he put it up again as it was, and today's **cathedral** testifies to Dol's former power. Inside glorious stained-glass windows illuminate the 300-foot-long nave. The stained-glass windows in the choir, dating from the end of the 13th century, show scenes of St. Samson and the first bishops of Dol, among others. Some charming old houses line the surrounding streets, particularly **Grand-Rue des Stuarts.**

François-René de Chateaubriand, most romantic of France's Romantic authors, lived for a time in his youth at **Combourg** castle. Surrounded by a park, its pepperpot towers reflected in the little "lake" below, the castle is melancholy, brooding, moody and austere. Chateaubriand's tyrannical father acquired it in 1761. You can visit (in season only) the tiny room up in the **Tour du Chat** that François-René occupied, as well as the **museum** of souvenirs in the former archives. For all lovers of Chateaubriand's writings, Combourg is a place of pilgrimage—if only for the stroll through the wood, round the gloomy but oh-so-romantic "pond", to the stone statue of the author by Boucher, shown, with top hat in hand, looking—inevitably—sad. **35**

Northern Coasts

So negative is the word "northern" in many people's minds that the *département* of Côtes-du-Nord toys with the idea of changing its name to Côtes-d'Armor. In fact, though, the stretch of coast from Saint-Brieuc to Morlaix has absolutely nothing to envy any other. Hydrangeas bloom everywhere. The pink of the granite gives the houses a tinge of something special, and the rugged rocks and boulders, sculpted by the elements, have taken on wondrous shapes—the Breton imagination needed no further encouragement to fabulate...

Saint-Brieuc and its Coast

Perched high on a promontory between the Gouët and Gouëdic rivers, the busy capital of the Côtes-du-Nord lies some 3 kilometres inland from Le Légué, its port. **Saint-Brieuc** is the essence of a country town: a few old, old houses, a pleasant pedestrians-only centre of town, a fortress-like cathedral, markets, good restaurants, and plenty of *pâtisseries* give it a cheerful, human feel. An invisible line running roughly between Saint-Brieuc and Vannes on the south coast separates French-speaking Brittany from the Breton-speaking section.

Following the shore from

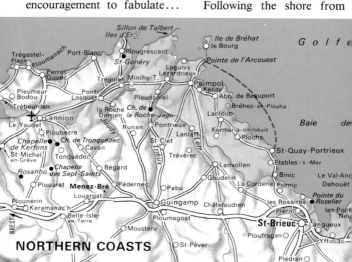

NORTHERN COASTS

Saint-Brieuc to Morlaix takes you along the Côte du Guëlo, the Côte de Granit Rose and Côte de Bruyères, within reach of a hinterland noted for its intimate, friendly scenery.

On the first part of the coast several resorts follow each other in rapid succession: BINIC, ETABLES-SUR-MER and **Saint-Quay-Portrieux,** with four beaches, two harbours (one for fishing boats, another for pleasure craft), a sailing club, casino, tennis courts and walks along the shore. You can make a brief incursion inland to tiny **Kermaria-an-Iskuit,** whose chapel has thought-provoking, 15th-century frescoes of the

Danse macabre. Hand in hand, red against black, 47 skeletal figures circle round the wooden ceiling, in the infernal Dance of Death. Everyone joins in—pope and king, merchant and monk, peasant and money-lender. Only the two lovers seem to be spared.

Further along, a stone's throw from the sea, stands the Premonstratensian **Abbey of Beauport** (just outside Paimpol). Few ruins are as evocative as these gaunt ivy-grown stones and solitary towering walls. Of the monastic buildings put up round 1200 by Alain de Penthièvre, you can visit the church, the Salle au Duc, the

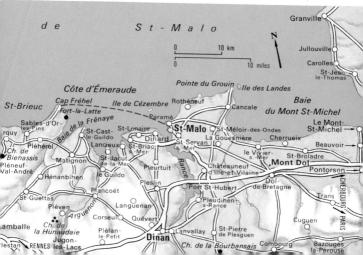

massive refectory and the long chapter-house.

Time has not been kind to **Paimpol,** famous of old for its cod-fishing fleets. The boats would put out to sea for months at a time, trawling in Icelandic and Newfoundland waters, many never to return. Dedicated today to oyster-raising and vegetable farming, the town serves as the terminus for ferries to the beautiful, car-free, quasi-Mediterranean island of **Bréhat,** just offshore, amid a sea bristling with reefs and islets.

Côte de Granit Rose

The violet-pink hue of the rock formations gives the Côte de Granit Rose its name. This scenic stretch of beach begins at l'Arcouest and continues west as far as Trébeurden, taking in Perros-Guirec, voted Brittany's favourite family beach. But first comes delightful **Tréguier** (population 3,000), situated on a hill 5 kilometres inland, at the confluence of the Guindy and Jaudy rivers.

No city is more "Breton" than Tréguier, no cathedral of Brittany's nine quite as beloved as its **Cathédrale Saint-Tugdual.** The church, built

Shellfish gatherers set out to scour the Côte du Granit Rose.

mostly between 1339 and 1468, is a masterpiece of delicacy. Three towers rise above the transept: the square 12th-century Tour Hastings (all that remains of an earlier edifice), the Gothic centrepiece, the Tour du Sanctuaire, and an openwork spire of 1787.

Inside, you'll be struck by the gloriously luminous nave (the glass is mostly modern Breton work). Each pair of pillars has a different design and colour of stone, corresponding to various different periods of construction. The cathedral honours St. Yves, patron saint of lawyers and native of Tréguier. On May 19, lawyers from around the world gather here to participate in the *pardon* of St. Yves, a traditional ceremony in which suppliants ask forgiveness for sins— or offer thanks for favours granted. Richly decorated chapels flank the aisle, particularly the vast **Chapelle Saint-Yves,** which contains the tomb of the saint, executed in 1420 and reconstructed in 1890. The little plaques around the saint's tomb bear messages of hope or gratitude, some in Breton. Elegant flamboyant granite arcades propped by buttresses surround the beautiful **cloister** (small entrance fee), a haven of hydrangeas—and peace.

The 19th-century philosopher and writer Ernest Renan, remembered for his efforts to reconcile science and religion, grew up in Tréguier. Visit his birthplace, the lovely wood-panelled 16th-century **Maison de Renan** in Rue Renan.

North of Tréguier at the Pointe du Château and Pors-Scarff, rock formations call to mind weird and wonderful animals of myth—a phenomenon that gets more and more marked as you continue along this wild coast.

Inland hub of the Côte de Granit Rose, **Lannion** symbolizes the new dynamism of Brittany, with its airport and telecommunications centre, set up in 1962. The Léguer flows calmly through the centre of town, flanked by the formal Quai d'Aiguillon. The market bustles round the quayside and sprawls up the side streets to the main square, **Place du Général-Leclerc,** with some superb medieval houses. The **Eglise de Brélévenez,** a Templars' church, stands at the top of a beautiful 142-step stairway. Vigorous, yet distinctly charming, Lannion makes as excellent a halt for shopping as for sightseeing.

From Lannion, other possibilities inland should be investigated: the romantic ruins of the **Château de Tonquédec,**

the 18th-century **Chapelle des Sept-Saints** (curious Islamo-Christian *pardon*), the gardens of the **Château de Rosambo** and that wild and lonely mount, the **Ménez-Bré.**

Back now to the coast, **Perros-Guirec,** some 12 kilometres north of Lannion, has not only managed to keep its Breton character but to develop its coastline harmoniously. The 1900-style villas stand amid luxuriant mimosas and hydrangeas, shaded by maritime

pines. The town proper begins around the **Rade** (roadstead) and its port—a real fishing port with plenty of anchorage for yachts. The centre of town lies uphill, spilling out into a commercial district that reaches down again to the beaches of Trestignel (smaller and more intimate) and **Trestraou.** The clean, pure sand sweeps round in front of the casino and congress hall, the big hotels and thalassotherapy centre. Away in the distance lie the Sept-Iles,

Silver sands of Perros-Guirec, Brittany's favourite family beach.

seven small islands forming an ornithological reserve (two-hour visits from Trestraou).

From Perros-Guirec, visit the hamlet of LA CLARTÉ, where the delightful pink-coloured **chapel,** Notre-Dame-de-la-Clarté, was put up on the very spot where a grateful seaman sighted land after a storm in the mid-16th-century. Take **41** the footpath, the **Sentier des Douaniers,** round from Perros through the bracken for some sensational views of the sea and the rocks, that the wind has sculpted into strange human or object forms such as a foot and a hat, and reach **Ploumanach,** where port, town and chapel cohabit amid the fantastic rocky chaos.

The coast road, the Corniche Bretonne (or, more prosaically, D.788), carries on to **Trégastel.** Mounds of huge rocks, in infernal disorder, lie everywhere, stacked crazily upon each other. Quite a startling change of scene occurs a few kilometres beyond, inland, as a huge white sphere, the radardome *(radôme)* of the **Pleumeur-Bodou** space telecommunications station that provided the first intercontinental television link via Telstar in July 1962, emerges from the bracken and broom. You can take a guided tour of the centre.

Finally **Trébeurden,** end-station of the Côte de Granit Rose, has all the trappings of a good beach resort, with two well-sited beaches (beaches facing south are rare in the north) ensconsed in greenery.

Côte des Bruyères

South of Trébeurden, the rock reverts to its usual grey-brown hue. Shrub and pine cling to the curtain of cliffs, while heather *(bruyères)* bedecks the open land.

Again, Lannion is best point of departure. The tiny road following the left bank of the River Léguer weaves its way through lovely countryside to the sweet hamlet of **Le Yaudet.** Its chapel, **Notre-Dame-du-Yaudet,** stands on top of a cliff that drops precipitously towards the mouth of the river. You'll like the touching naïve sculpture of Christ's birth inside.

Further west lies a remarkable beach, the **Lieue de Grève.** So firm, so broad and so flat is the three-mile expanse of sand that horse races are held on it. Depending on the tide, it's about a mile wide. Two small resorts stand at either end of the beach: **Saint-Michel-en-Grève** and SAINT-EFFLAM. You will be moved by Saint-Michel's church and cemetery right beside the sea, lashed by the waves.

The spectacular **Corniche de l'Armorique** rises and falls as it winds round the wooded Pointe de Plestin and on to **Locquirec,** friendly fishing port-cum-family beach resort. The town, technically in Finistère, lies on a sheltered peninsula, its port protected by a jetty.

Northern Finistère

Finistère, Brittany's western-most *département,* is split about half-way down by the River Elorn, between Léon, the district to the north and Cornouaille (Cornwall) to the south. Parts are highly fertile, parts arid and hilly. Here the coast is at its most rugged, the sea at its most exhilarating, awe-inspiring and perilous— hard to believe on a warm, calm day at one of the southern beaches. If the shape of Finistère can be compared to a roaring lion with an open mouth, its lower jaw would be Cap Sizun, its tongue Crozon and the upper jaw, the Côte des Abers, with its capital Morlaix.

Morlaix

Emblem of the city, Morlaix's **viaduct** straddles the valley, casting its shadow like up-turned fingers over the little town clustered below. Round the estuary at portside huddle the wealthy merchants' houses, and a fleet of (mostly) pleasure boats lies at anchor.

   The town early on enjoyed the mixed blessings of prosperity of a rich merchant town (subsequently Brest, under Louis XIV, stole its limelight). For in 1522, the envious British, tipped off that Morlaix's

men were absent one day, raided and pillaged the town. Distracted by the pleasures of the wine cellars, they were unprepared when the Morlaisians returned and delivered them a sound thrashing.

The **Maison de la Duchesse Anne** (33, rue du Mur) is Morlaix's greatest attraction; its direct connection with the Breton heroine may be tenuous, but the 15th-century corbelled mansion (restored last century) is certainly the type she would have seen during her tour of the province's highspots in 1505. The façade bristles all over with statues of saints and *grotesques,* while inside, in a skylighted courtyard surrounded by galleries, a remarkable staircase corkscrews its way around a tall wooden pillar.

Morlaix Area

From Morlaix, a beautiful road winds along the estuary to fashionable CARANTEC at the mouth of the Bay of Morlaix. Neighbouring **Saint-Pol-de-Léon** has two claims to fame, beyond its pleasant, deeply Breton feel. Capital of the rich agricultural region known as the *Ceinture Dorée* (Golden Belt), it supplies most of Europe with artichokes, as well as a sizeable quantity of potatoes, asparagus, spring onions and cauliflower. In the flat fields of Léon, artichokes, monstrous spiky balls atop tall stalks, vie for attention with the church and chapel belfries peeking over every horizon. Saint-Pol-de-Léon has, however, two silhouettes that not only can be seen from far and wide, but that symbolize Brittany.

The former **cathedral,** set sideways onto the main square, dates back to the 13th and 14th centuries. The nave, built of limestone, betrays a distinctly Norman influence, while local Breton granite was employed for the façade. Carved wooden **stalls** dignify the interior, depicting scenettes and personages. On the left, just behind the choir stalls, you'll see a rather grisly collection of **skulls** *(chefs),* 35 in all, belonging to three centuries of town notables. St. Pol's bones are kept in a gilded bronze **reliquary** opposite.

Rue du Général-Leclerc, the lively main artery lined with old houses, links the former cathedral to the **Kreisker** (Chapelle Notre-Dame-du-Kreisker), the 14th-century chapel whose marvellous 15th-century belfry soars up 253 feet. The Gothic belfry, with its slender elongated steeple flanked way above by four turrets, has served as a model for many a

Breton church. The windy view from the top of the tower encompasses the town, the vast fields of artichokes, the Corniche de l'Armorique and the isle of Batz in a dazzling sea.

Artichokes were behind the development of **Roscoff** into an important car ferry port; it was only a step, after all, from transporting artichokes and spring vegetables *(primeurs)* to transporting tourists. Right down at the old port, a small watchtower stands on the spot where Mary Queen of Scots landed in 1548, at the tender age of 5½ ... to be married to François, Dauphin of France, at the even more tender age of

Saint-Thégonnec's calvary casts drama of the Passion, Breton-style.

3½. Apart from the old port and the cross-channel port, Roscoff has a fishing port (lobster and crayfish), while a long snaking jetty serves as the terminus for ferries to BATZ, a 15-minute ride away. The sea enters into every aspect of Roscoff's activity. Apart from a famous thalassotherapy clinic, the town boasts a prominent marine biological laboratory, and, directly below, the fascinating **Aquarium Charles-Pérez** with a display of Channel sea-life.

Parish Close Road

Nothing is more quintessentially Breton than the parish close *(enclos paroissial)*, an architectural ensemble encompassing church, cemetery, charnel house and calvary, grouped around a square and entered via a triumphal arch. In a morning's tour from Morlaix, you can take in the top three (among scores)—Saint-Thégonnec, Guimiliau and Lampaul-Guimiliau—signposted as the "Circuit des Trois Enclos".

Saint-Thégonnec, the best all-round example, represents the ultimate flowering of the art. The triumphal arch sets the tone for the majestic **calvary** of 1610. Forty-odd figures dressed in the costume of the Henri IV period are remarkably expressive and the scenes telling. Notice, for instance, the angels collecting Christ's blood and the roped hands of the blindfolded Christ; his tormentor, in breeches, is thought to be Henri IV himself. Below, a niche contains a stumpy, robed St. Thégonnec with a wolf harnessed to a cart (the saint's speciality was taming wild animals).

The exceptionally elaborate **ossuary,** now a chapel, has pride of place. The façade is pure Breton Renaissance with neat Corinthian columns, lanterns, niches and caryatids. The church is notable for its 1683 pulpit—with a canopy of 1722 capped by the Angel of Judgement blowing his trumpet.

Undoubtedly the glory of **Guimiliau** resides in its **calvary,** where over 200 figures from the Old and New Testaments go about their affairs, with Breton legends and history mixed in. Renaissance grace and elegance here get the upper hand from the wild nightmares and superstition of the Middle Ages. Look for the figure of Katell Gollet (Catherine the Lost), a servant girl who flirted with the devil, shown being hurtled into hell. Superb tiny "scenettes" ring the porch which contains lovely granite statues of Christ and the Apostles. Inside the church, eight spiral columns uphold the mighty canopy of the intricately carved wooden baptistry of 1675, quivering with decorations—note the birds nibbling grapes.

A lightning bolt struck the church of **Lampaul-Guimiliau** in 1809, toppling its proud tower. But the **church** remains impressive within. The 16th-century rood beam spanning the nave bears sculptures of the

A parish close, complete: church and calvary, ossuary and arch stand together at Guimiliau.

The Parish Close

Just as kings and dukes vied to build castles, one more beautiful than the next, so, on a more limited scale, the wealthy merchants of Brittany competed to erect the most impressive parish closes. In the years following the integration of Brittany into France, between 1550 and 1560, construction reached its zenith. In Finistère, at the limit between Léon and Cornouaille, even the tiniest *commune* had its close.

Situated right in the centre of the village, the parish close with its cemetery and charnel house (bodies were disinterred and the bones placed here to make room in the graveyard for new arrivals) formed a sort of community of the dead. For death *(Ankou)* is a perennial Breton obsession.

Entry was through a triumphal arch, since through it one passes into the kingdom of death, to life eternal. The calvary, certainly the most original feature, embodies in granite Breton religious fervour. The basic elements are everywhere the same: a central cross, flanked by the crosses of the two thieves, rises up above a group of horsemen (Roman guards); below, the Virgin Mary holds up the body of a recumbent Jesus, removed from the cross. On the dais are friezes of personages, humble and noble, from saints, soldiers and politicians to executioners and torturers. If you want to visualize the Brittany of 400 years ago, it's all there—in stone.

sibyls (chancel side) and scenes of the Passion. Look out for the famous representation of the Flagellation: a red-shirted sadist with a whip and another with cudgels delight in attacking Christ, bound to a tree. If the triumphal arch and sober mini-calvary are relatively unimpressive, the ossuary (1667) has interesting sculptures.

We'll meet other *enclos* later —and some fine ones—but first turn back to the coast, growing ever more dramatic, and its hinterland.

Côte des Abers

Swept by the west wind, this wild, relatively little-developed coastal area stretches round from Saint-Pol-de-Léon to Pointe de Saint-Mathieu, west of Brest. The word *aber* means estuary. Beaches are few and far between, but there's plenty of savage scenery—and treacherous seas in which many a ship has come to grief amid islets and reefs.

First stop on the coast is

Brignogan-Plage, scattered with rocks and boulders. Continuing west you'll see Phare de la Vierge, a lighthouse visible for miles around. The views over **Aber-Wrac'h Estuary** are glorious: dark rocks, gorse-covered slopes, occasional farm plots, sinuous roads. The **Aber-Benoît,** four miles deep, splays out in all directions. The river may be less grandiose than its sister but picturesque even so as you cross over the bridge of TRÉGLONOU. Women in clogs and weatherbeaten, worn crosses and calvaries along the road attest to the traditional nature of this part of Brittany— an area that musters many Breton-speakers.

The beach resort of PORSPODER becomes positively magical at night as you watch the ballet of lighthouse beams. The road follows the Aber Ildut round through **Brélès:** here (technically) Channel and Atlantic meet. Soon, from the Pointe de Corsen, most westerly point in France, the isles of Molène and mysterious, wild, windswept **Ouessant** (Ushant) come into view.

Sailors dread the surly seas off this part of the coast: countless disasters have occurred in the Passage du Fromveur between the two islands. (Safe) trips by boat or hydrofoil leave from **Le Conquet,** main port on the Côte des Abers. Unexceptional as a town, its pleasant harbour in a well-sheltered bay is dotted with rows of blue fishnets for crayfish and lobster, Le Conquet's great specialities.

Just south lies **Pointe de Saint-Mathieu,** one of Brittany's most soul-stirring sights. A legend explains the name: sailors from Léon, carrying the head of St. Matthew to the monastery here, ran aground on the reef off the point, but thanks to the holy relic with them, their path was cleared. St. Tanguy erected a monastery on the point in the 6th century. The infinitely moving **ruins** of the church—90 feet up from the waves, whipped by the howling winds and drenched by the spray—stand locked in mortal combat with the eroding wind.

Sights Inland

For all the glories of the coast, a few highspots inland should not be missed.

South-west of Saint-Pol-de-Léon nestles **Kerjean,** part-medieval fortress, part-Renaissance château. A fire in 1710 caused terrible damage, but enough remains to give an excellent picture of how Brittany's privileged half lived from **49** the 16th to 18th centuries. The kitchen with its huge chimneys, the dining room, salons, bedrooms and the enchanting miniature **chapel** set the style of life at the château.

West again is little LE FOLGOËT, site of one of Brittany's great churches, **Notre-Dame-de-Folgoët** (1423), and scene of one of the most important *pardons* in the country (p. 94). The north tower, at 180 feet, with its graceful façade, dominates the dolls' houses that ring the esplanade below. Inside note the superb, lace-like, dark granite **rood screen.**

In Breton *Folgoët* means "madman of the wood": sometime in the 1350s, Salaün, a simple soul who lived in the trunk of a hollow oak, went around crying the Madonna's name. When he died and was buried, a lily grew out of his mouth: on its petals in gold letters was the name of the Virgin Mary. Word of the miracle got around, and the flow of pilgrims began—and it just happened to coincide with Breton victory at Auray in 1364. The dukes quickly recuperated the event for political ends. But they had also put up the funds...

The Far West

Go West! The Far West is where you go for dramatic sea effects, for the austere scenery of land's end, Pointe du Raz, and some enviable beaches like Bénodet, Beg-Meil and Loctudy. The Far West has Brittany's chief naval port, Brest, and its biggest strawberry-growing area, Plougastel. The region also encompasses the deeply traditional Pays Bigouden, with its typical costumes

Contemplating the points and peninsulas of Brittany's Far West.

and customs, and the gentle, smiling countryside round Pont-Aven and Quimperlé.

Brest and its Roadstead

In 1631 Cardinal de Richelieu designated Brest as France's major naval base. He could hardly have chosen a better natural harbour. The roadstead, vast enough to shelter a whole fleet, narrows at the Goulet de Brest to provide excellent protection. Alas, it proved too good a site: most of

Brest's accumulated history was destroyed in Allied bombardments of World War II. Rebuilt with broad straight avenues and big squares, the post-war city of 200,000 is a thoroughly businesslike place.

Nowadays, the most striking sights in **Brest** are undoubtedly the panoramic views out over the roadstead. From the superb **Cours Dajot** promenade (1768), watch boats of all sizes coming and going. The view sweeps around from the yacht harbour

by the Elorn Estuary to the commercial harbour, with its gesticulating cranes, to beyond the castle, in the inner harbour, where the French fleet lies at anchor. (Only French nationals can visit the vast naval base, situated alongside the River Penfeld and out around the bay.)

Be sure to see the fascinating **Musée du Vieux-Brest** (on the right bank near Recouvrance Bridge), an exhibition of documents and pictures that brings old Brest to life, particularly its former "model" penal colony.

Continue east now beside the River Elorn to **Landerneau** (20 km.), one of the great crossroads of the province, with the first and only bridge for miles. The **Pont de Rohan** (1510), the oldest inhabited bridge in Europe, spans the Elorn, a broad splashing river; astride the bridge, two rows of elegant, shingle-covered houses and a mini-manor glare across at each other. Each side of the river has its *quai,* its old houses of warm yellow stone and its church (both splendid).

Facing Brest, within the roadstead, is the **Presqu'île de Plougastel.** Little strawberry bushes cover the length and breadth of the peninsula. But for artlovers there's an even greater draw: the **calvary** at PLOU-GASTEL-DAOULAS, one of the greatest of them all, standing alone in the great square. It was built between 1602 and 1604 to commemorate the end of a plague; some 150 figures heave, sigh, grovel and gesticulate, seized in motion almost as at Pompeii.

Daoulas is notable for its old **abbey,** founded in the period of Breton migration in the 5th and 6th centuries. Three sides of the arcaded Romanesque cloister still stand in a lovely setting; the (restored) arcades are formed of Kersanton stone columns, six feet tall. Note in particular the capitals, as well as the delightful central octagonal basin of 1352 with geometrical designs. Ring the bell to enter.

The little town of LE FAOU lies tucked away at the easternmost end of the Brest roadstead, its main street emerging straight from the 16th century.

The Crozon Peninsula

A superb corniche road leads from Le Faou to the Crozon Peninsula, providing lush green views as it follows the Faou Estuary. Away in the not-so-distant distance looms the unmistakable silhouette of Ménez-Hom, the last hiccup of the Montagnes Noires.

Like a crooked little finger, the northernmost prong of the

peninsula doubles back on itself towards the mainland. Sheltered by wooded hills, **Landévennec** faces Le Faou and the Aulne Estuary. It's worth a visit for its old abbey, ancestor of all Brittany's monasteries, founded by St. Guénolé in the 5th century. The abbey became the storehouse of Breton tradition and religious and intellectual achievement until its destruction. At the edge of the village proper, the **ruins** (mostly 11th century) stand out against the sea, poignant and evocative, but very fragmentary. The interesting little **museum** beside has a diorama show illustrating the history of the monastery.

South-west lies **Morgat**, one of the most agreeable resorts in the area. The little town fronts a sheltered, horseshoe-shaped pure sand beach.

From Morgat you can reach **Cap de la Chèvre** (Goat Cape) by car, by boat—introducing you to the otherwise inaccessible **grotto** called Grotte du Charivari—or by clifftop footpath (8 km.). The cape rises 300 feet sheer above sea level and projects out into the Bay of Douarnenez. At the tip of the cape, children sell tempting chunks of amethyst. Birds are in their element.

Pointe de Dinan, accessible by road from Morgat, has cliffs as jagged and abrupt as any. You positively feel the swirling currents below.

Camaret had a difficult past as an outpost for Brest; its present is scarcely easy, either, with the crisis in the lobster-fishing industry. The incongruous **Château Vauban** (designed by the military architect Vauban late in the 17th century) today houses an amusing naval museum *(Musée Historique et Naval).*

At the end of the 18th century, 700 menhirs stood on the site of **Lagatjar,** just west; today 143 line up amid the daisies. Stout, mysterious, a bit the worse for wear, the stones form intersecting lines, providing one of the best examples in Brittany of an alignment (see box p. 65).

From some 200 feet up at the **Pointe de Penhir,** contemplate the roaring seas and the beaches with their puppet-like humans. Straggling out in front, like peas in a pod, is Les Tas de Pois, a group of five or six rugged blocks studding the sea, to the greater joy of seabirds of all colours and species.

Last of Crozon's views is the **Pointe des Espagnols.** As you follow the road, faithfully hugging the coast, you'll marvel at the variety of the panorama of the roadstead and its maritime traffic.

Land's End

The next (major) peninsula down, Presqu'île de Sizun has the most famous landmark of all: Pointe du Raz. When the sea is fully unleashed, the thunder of the waves here can be felt all the way to Quimper, nearly 20 miles away.

The Bay of Douarnenez separates the Sizun and Crozon Peninsulas. Situated beside the bay, SAINTE-ANNE-LA-PALUD comes to life one day a year, the last Sunday in August, when the *pardon* takes place. The townsfolk wear local dress, and the women their *coiffes*. Bearing banners, they head for the 19th-century chapel of Sainte-Anne-la-Palud, isolated amid the dunes.

In summer, nearby **Locronan** bustles with life. A town of artisans since time immemorial, Locronan was known for the production of sailcloth. Nowadays, in the main square and in side-streets, artisans are still active but at jewellery- and pottery-making, granite carving, glass-blowing, and silk-painting. Art exhibitions are organized, painters appear, weaving demonstrations are given, music festivals put on... When you see the charm of this picture-postcard village with its granite façades, you'll realize why.

Find time nevertheless to peek into the **Eglise Saint-Ronan** on the main square, and particularly its side-chapel, the **Chapelle du Pénity** (1510–14) with its superb tomb of St. Ronan.

Douarnenez overlooks the great bay of the same name. It's essentially a fishing and canning town (one of Brittany's biggest for sardines, but also for tunny fish, mackerel and shellfish). Stroll around the Rosmeur port area and attend a

Low tide on the low-lying Island of Sein leaves this sailor high and dry.

fish auction *(criée)* if you have the chance. Try and be present when the fleets leave or return; and at least take advantage of the opportunity to sample crabs, oysters, *palourdes,* shrimps, mussels and crayfish.

The pretty port of **Audierne** (22 km. from Douarnenez) forms a horseshoe around both shores of the Goyen Estuary, a mile from the sea. Crayfish, lobster and tunny fish boats bob in the harbour. And yet how many tragedies has it seen, how many seamen have left in these frail barques never to return…

Taking the road from Audierne up the arm of the peninsula, the scenery is much the same—rough and ready, but 55

Where is Is?

The legendary city of Is (or Ys) lay somewhere in the Bay of Douarnenez. King Gradlon reigned over the town, so the story goes, but the debauchery of his daughter Dahut brought the wrath of God down upon it. Gradlon, warned to flee by St. Guénolé of Landévennec, dragged Dahut away on the back of his horse. However the weight of her sins forced him to abandon her, and Dahut (and Is) sank for ever beneath the waves.

Tidal waves have occurred at various points along the Breton coast, and it's not impossible a wave in the 4th or 5th century did in fact engulf a town of some size in the area. But such is the stuff of legends, too good for the Bretons to let by . . .

green—until you reach the last real village before the Pointe du Raz, PLOGOFF, where vegetation gets sparser; for the ancients, the eerie, bleak and barren terrain signalled the end of the known world. Nowadays land's end, the **Pointe du Raz**, suggests Piccadilly at rush hour —thanks to traffic jams, a rash of souvenir-sellers, tourist touts and restaurants. The hour-long guided tours of the cape (with an accredited guide) are popular and worthwhile as you clamber down into the hissing, hellish Enfer de Plogoff. Be sure to wear sturdy shoes and keep to the paths and railings. The flat, desolate and tragic **Island of Sein** lies a few miles over the seas, deceptively calm.

Barely less impressive, but fractionally less frequented is the **Pointe du Van** just north; the humble Chapelle de Saint-They dominates the maritime scene of jagged rocks, swirling seagulls, strangely shaped rocks (they all have names), waves, lighthouses and windswept moorland.

From Pointe du Van, the northern coastal road rises above the shoreline at an average 180 feet, providing some splendid views of the Bay of Douarnenez. Look out for the side road leading to the **Réserve Ornithologique du Cap-Sizun**, open from March to the end of August. A guided tour of the reserve allows you to see the birds (puffins, herring gulls, choughs, razorbills, fulmers, petrels, cormorants) in their natural habitat, undisturbed. Take binoculars.

South now of Audierne, and following its bay, you meet

The coiffes of Bigouden, a woman's crowning glory, don't prevent an exchange of the latest gossip.

mostly barren, open country-side. Red earth trickles right down to the sea; tiny, stone-walled fields snuggle up against the wind as roller after roller crashes in on the shingly beach; and cows, indifferent to sea and wind, munch sparse grass.

Be careful on this inhospitable shoreline; the sea here is cruel and treacherous; don't try swimming without taking advice.

Pays Bigouden

This region of 24 communes hangs like a beard from the jaw of Cap Sizun. The Pays Bigouden takes its name from the monstrously tall, pointed lace *coiffes* worn by the women: *begou* = point, *den* = person. The Pays Bigouden is a world apart, its landscapes secretive and severe, its people rugged personalities.

Start with its "capital", **Pont-l'Abbé** (some 32 km. from Audierne), a town of 8,000 inhabitants. The **Musée Bigouden** in the dungeon of the château (what is left of it), reveals aspects of life in the Bigouden ports, as well as of the countryside. Though seamen and farmers lived side by side, the two often ignored each other. On display are models of fishing boats, furniture and magnificent costumes.

LOCTUDY, down at the mouth of the River de Pont-l'Abbé, has a busy port, with sailing clubs and good family beaches. But its true claim to fame is its **Romanesque church,** very rare in Brittany and one of the best preserved examples. Although the façade was spoiled during reconstruction in the 18th century, the harmonious interior retains its 12th-century aspect. Topping the pillars, green with age, are capitals decorated in Celtic style with under-and-over doodle patterns—some of which turn into human figures.

The town of **Penmarch** lies a short distance inland. Formerly the Penmarch region was one of the richest areas in Brittany thanks to its cod-fishing industry, and the 16th-century church of **Saint-Nonna** reflects the glory that was. The elegant porch, decorated with ship motifs, testifies to the wealth and interests of the church's benefactors, ship owners all.

West of town, note an unmistakable silhouette: the 15th-century chapel of **Notre-Dame-de-la-Joie** projects out literally into the sea, protected from its battering by a wall.

Saint-Guénolé sits at the head of the Peninsula of Penmarch (literally "horse's head"), facing the unbridled

Atlantic. The ancients settled in the area, as is testified by the exhibits of the **Musée Préhistorique.** There's a garden-full of megalithic replicas from all over the area, and plenty of Bronze Age weapons, tools and ornaments inside.

North at **Pointe de la Torche** the wind blows hard and strong, filling the windsurfers' sails. Earth, sky and sea seem to come together in moody harmony, and the salty tang in the air invigorates.

Just north-east and barely a few hundred yards from the sea huddles the chapel of **Notre-Dame-de-Tronoën.** Here, isolated amid the dunes, stands a **calvary,** the oldest (1450)—and maybe the most moving—of all Breton calvaries. It relates incidents in the life of Jesus in a simple, naïve way. Time, wind and weather have battered the lower of two levels of statues and erased some faces, but many of the 100-odd personages retain their fresh, frank expressions.

Brittany's Cornwall

Quimper is the treasurehouse of the Bretons' values and traditions. It's also capital of Cornouaille, a district named by the nostalgic Celts after their native Cornwall in England.

The town's beginnings go back to prehistoric times; the Romans set up camp here at the point where the rivers Steir and Odet meet. The **Cathédrale Saint-Corentin,** named after the patron saint of Quimper, represents one of Brittany's proudest achievements in religious architecture. Work on the building began around 1240 and went on for the best part of 600 years. The graceful towers, tall, weatherbeaten and delicately decorated all over, must be—so one imagines—the oldest part of all; in fact they're newest (1856)—the granite eroded and the originals needed replacement.

Inside, the nave appears to curve in the middle where the choir begins, an effect that comes from an error in calculations or early construction problems. Up above and all around light filters beautifully through the remarkable 15th-century **stained-glass windows,** bringing to life a multitude of Breton saints and sinners. Note the beautiful statues and **effigies** in the side chapels, particularly the alabaster 15th-century St. John the Baptist.

Two interesting museums stand either side of the cathedral. The **Musée Breton** is housed in the former Bishopric, a lovely Renaissance building that slots into the city walls. Its **59**

miniature garden, full of cathedral "spare parts" and statues, provides a preview of the fascinating collection of objects relating to Breton history, folklore and customs.

The **Musée des Beaux-Arts,** on the other side of the cathedral, displays an admirable collection of Breton, French, Flemish and Dutch artists. There are works by members of Brittany's own Pont-Aven School—but not by its founder, Gauguin.

Now plunge into Quimper proper. **Rue Kéréon** leads through the heart of town to the picturesque **Place Terre-au-Duc** (literally "Duke's Land"): in Quimper's medieval heyday the Bishop of Cornouaille owned the walled city, while the Duke of Brittany laid claim to the area outside. Streets and narrow alleyways *(venelles)* have evocative names related to the trades of the artisans who operate here. Half-timbered, cantilevered houses lean out over passers-by. Wooden figures leer and jeer.

Twenty-odd bridges, some stone, some iron, some traffic-bearing, others pedestrian, cross

Medieval Rue Kéréon heads straight for Quimper's cathedral, topped by legendary King Gradlon.

the Odet all the way down the main quayside arteries. On either side of the river, impressive town houses and flowered ramparts line the quay up to Locmaria. Here the Odet opens out, forms a harbour and becomes subject to the tides.

Ceramics incorporating clay from the riverbank have been produced in Quimper for nearly three centuries. In about 1690, one Jean-Baptiste Bousquet started a factory here that expanded with the arrival of a Rouen potter who married into the family. In the 19th century a typical local style featuring scenes of Breton peasants in blues, reds and greens was developed. A factory visit is instructive and amusing—and the chances are you'll take a piece away with you.

Turning resolutely south now, you reach, sheltered behind the Penmarch Peninsula, one of the beaches that has made the fame of Brittany—**Bénodet.** Its reputation and prosperity are reflected in the figures: 2,000 inhabitants in winter, 30,000 plus in summer. Bénodet enjoys the full favours of a gentle climate—it's all aflower with a Mediterranean-type vegetation. There's a steepish sandy beach facing south, and all the requisite installations and beach possibilities. **61**

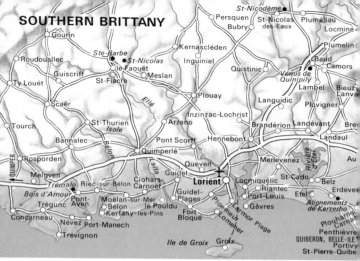

SOUTHERN BRITTANY

The sands follow on round without interruption to another of the great beach resorts of the area, smaller, more intimate, with noble villas secluded in the pines. In **Beg-Meil** palm trees, mimosa and aloes prosper. The Grande Plage (beach) gives on to the Atlantic Ocean, but a small beach on the Baie de la Forêt follows the jagged bay to FOUESNANT and across to Concarneau.

Concarneau is one of the best preserved, most picturesque walled towns in Brittany (if, alas, somewhat over-commercialized). It's also the province's biggest tunny fishing port, and no mean sar-

dine producer either. Actually, though, Concarneau is two towns: a modern one, relatively unattractive—but with a colourful and impressive fleet in the harbour—and a picturesque old city (the *Ville Close*) living its own life on a small island in full view of the fishing fleets.

From the quayside, Place Jean-Jaurès faces the old city's solid walls, shaped like an inverted comma and approached by a small bridge, the only entrance. First walk along the 14th-century **ramparts,** enclosing three-quarters of the Ville Close. At the start of the busy **Rue Vauban,** backbone of the town, is the fascinating **Musée**

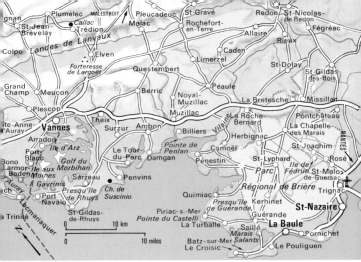

de la Pêche, devoted to the history of the town and its fishing activity. Displays include some 20 tanks of fish of all shapes and colours, models of the different fishing craft and fishing techniques.

Take advantage of the chance to watch Concarneau's traditional *criée* (fish auction), held at the Quai Carnot from about 6.30 to 11 a.m.

A small Breton town gave its name to one of the great art movements of the 19th century, the School of Pont-Aven. If the painter Paul Gauguin chose **Pont-Aven** in 1886, he had his reasons. On an overcrowded summer day it's not always ob-

vious what precisely they were. Still you'll agree that the kernel of the village, where the stream hurtling down over the rocks meets the mill and the inn of Moulin de Rosmadec, is infinitely charming.

If you want to pursue Gauguin's track, follow the signs at the top of the village up through the Bois d'Amour to the 16th-century **Chapelle de Trémalo.** Gauguin used the Christ inside as a model for his *Yellow Christ*. At Nizon stands an unusual, weatherworn **calvary** that Gauguin transformed into his *Green Christ*.

The very name of BÉLON **63**

means oysters; it has become synonymous with a specific type of flat oyster—the most highly rated. A tiny village in a lovely wooded site on the broad River Bélon, it's just the place for a *dégustation,* a tasting. You can see the oyster beds on the north bank at low tide.

Two gentle rivers, the Ellé and Isole, come together and form a third, the Laïta. At the junction sits **Quimperlé**, a charming township where salmon fishermen, oblivious of the heavy traffic, line the banks of the two streams as they tumble downwards, passing on through the town. Visit the impressive rounded 12th-century **Église Sainte-Croix,** quite a surprise in the context (its origins are thought to go back to the Templars, although much restored), and stroll round the lower and upper towns with some lovely old houses.

At the mouth of the Laïta lies LE POULDU. After Gauguin settled here in 1889, the town followed the classic ascension of fishing village to cosmopolitan resort. The coast road travels past GUIDEL-PLAGE and its futuristic, sun-trap houses, to FORT-BLOQUÉ, on an island bristling with rocks, linked by a causeway to the mainland; it comes to an end almost at LARMOR-PLAGE, beside Lorient.

Menhir Country

If anything symbolizes Brittany in the popular imagination, it is Morbihan's megalithic remains. And no part of the province has so many as Carnac and the Quiberon area. But there's another side to this region, where sailors and swimmers, sun-lovers and sports enthusiasts congregate on warm sandy beaches.

Lorient originated as base of the French East India Company. Towards the end of the 18th century, however, France lost its Indian possessions and the company was ruined. It was Napoleon who first gave the port a military role—a role it could, as events turned out, have done without. For Lorient suffered during World War II more than practically any other town in Brittany. Reconstructed in its entirety with controversial results, the brisk, businesslike port and naval dockyard bustles with activity. Lorient is, moreover, the second fishing port in France. To see the fishing industry in action, it's worth going down to the Port de Keroman in the morning before 11 a.m.

Jealously, from the other side of the Blavet and Scorff Estuaries, Lorient's former rival **Port-Louis** gazes back at the victor; Port-Louis housed the original East India Company. Now it stares forlornly out to sea, its fortifications and citadel virtually intact—if all but deserted.

Carnac

You might drive straight through ERDEVEN blindly—until you find yourself on a busy road in the middle of row after serried row of stones, erect amid the gorse. The **Alignements de Kerzerho** number over 1,000 stones aligned over an area of nearly a mile.

You have in fact reached Europe's biggest and most impressive concentration of megalithic remains. By the time you get to **Carnac,** you'll have doubtless seen plenty of menhirs and dolmens. But nothing will quite have prepared you for the sight of Carnac's megalithic monuments.

The alignments consist of three main fields a few hundred yards outside the town proper: **Le Ménec,** the biggest, has 1,099 menhirs in 12 rows (plus 70 menhirs in a cromlech that encompasses part of the hamlet of Le Ménec). The field of **Kermario,** 200 yards away, has a dolmen and 1,029 menhirs in 10 rows. Among them is the menhir called the Giant of Manio: shaped like a clenched fist,

Megaliths

Boulders were the building blocks of the megalithic world. They were used to create all sorts of structures, each with its own name.

The **menhir,** a single upright stone, varies in size from small to colossal (350 tons). Menhirs were often arranged in rows called **alignments.** They could also be set up in a circle to form the structure known as a **cromlech.**

A chamber comprised of flat slabs of stone is called a **dolmen.** When covered over with earth, it is referred to as a **tumulus.** If stones, rather than earth, were heaped on top, it is a **cairn.**

Dolmens were usually approached down a tunnel formed by stones which could also stand as a separate structure—in which case it becomes a **covered alleyway** *(allée couverte).*

Often rather than remove them, subsequent "conquerors" turned menhirs to their own purposes, Christianizing them with a cross.

it stands some 20 feet high, dwarfing everyone. Finally comes the **Kerlescan** alignment, in some respects the most moving. Its 594 menhirs are the most unified and have the biggest specimens.

65

Legend has it that this is, in fact, a frozen army; once a year, in the depths of night, so the story goes, the stones rise up and march. The menhirs are best seen at sunrise or sunset, or in the hazy morning light, when they loom up through the wisps of mist. No one quite knows why they are here; it's fair to surmise, however, that they had some kind of divine ritual purpose. To transport the boulders required considerable social organization; and when you see the size and imagine the weight, quite some strength.

The alignments weren't, however, put up in a night, but rather in spurts over a thousand or two years (an average of about one stone a year) sometime between 5500 and 3500 B.C. The overall impression Carnac leaves is somewhat like that of the cities of the Mayas: the mysterious disappearance of a civilization that is trying to pass on a message.

Half a mile north-east of Carnac, on a rise, stands the **Tumulus Saint-Michel,** thought to have been built around 3000 B.C.; visitors creep through the long low corridors of this tomb complex, about 400 feet long and 40 feet high, to view tiny burial chambers illuminated by a guide brandishing a flash-light. Most of the best finds

The fields around Carnac are littered with megaliths of all shapes.

Le Rouzic, a Breton who first assisted Miln at the age of 10, started researching the prehistoric sites in the area in the 1860s. They built up the nucleus of a collection of prehistoric tools and works of art, since completed with fascinating new material.

In town, see the 17th-century church of **Saint-Cornély.** The paintings in the vaults (a coin in the slot puts on the light) poetically illustrate the acts of St. Cornély. The saint, who was particularly associated with horned animals, peers out from a niche in the façade, framed by two oxen.

Carnac Area

Carnac is decidedly multi-faceted. **Carnac-Plage,** turning its back on the megalithic world and on Carnac town, has come into its own as a health resort-cum-thalassotherapy centre; the long beach curves round and down, beneath a pleasant promenade and a lively back-scene. With a mile of fine, firm, gently sloping sand facing due south and a good yacht harbour, and with all the beach pleasures you could wish for, it's hardly surprising this has become one of the top resorts of the Morbihan region.

Nearby **La Trinité-sur-Mer** has its oyster beds down the

from here made their way to museums in either Carnac or Vannes. After a visit, climb above the tumulus to the **Chapelle Saint-Michel** and take in the beautiful view over the bristling megalithic world below, and beyond to the Quiberon Peninsula and to the wide open sea.

Carnac is called the prehistoric capital of the world, and to complete one's view and knowledge of prehistory, a visit to the **Musée Préhistorique** is a must. Miln, a Scotsman, and

Crach Estuary and some lovely beaches, but it has a greater claim to fame as a yacht centre. Facilities for yachtsmen are some of the best in Brittany. The town slopes down to the estuary; from the Pont de Kerisper there's a good view of the array of masts echoing the narrow gaunt houses.

Auray (13 km. inland) is an unpretentious town where the tragedies of bygone years are easily forgotten in the delights of the warm, homely countryside all around. Charles de Blois, champion of the French, was killed outside in 1364 by the troops of Jean I de Montfort, backed by the English. Thus the duchy remained Breton a while longer.

Most visitors desert Auray proper for the Promenade du Loch, leading to the **Port de Saint-Goustan** at the head of the River Auray. The American patriot Benjamin Franklin landed at this spot on December 4, 1776; an ageing gentleman of 70, he was on his way to drum up French support for the American War of Independence. Saint-Goustan is at first too good to be true, but the medieval houses around **Place Saint-Sauveur** are perfectly genuine and the restored church is mainly 15th and 16th century.

Six kilometres inland from Auray at **Sainte-Anne-d'Auray** is one of Brittany's most sacred spots—and certainly one where the *pardon* finds its greatest fervour (Pardon of St. Anne, July 26). In 1623, St. Anne appeared in a vision to Yves Nicolazic, a local peasant, and told him to put up a sanctuary where a chapel had been destroyed by the barbarians. When, two years later, Nicolazic dug up a statue of St. Anne on the site, the sceptical clergy had to react. A chapel was built in the same year (since demolished) and a convent *(Couvent des Carmes)* set up nearby, which today constitutes the only vestige of the 17th-century buildings. The vast, rather cold Renaissance-style basilica was put up between 1866 and 1873. Inside, in a little box, is all that remains of the original statue, burned in 1790—a splinter of the face. The astonishing **treasury,** in a wing of the convent adjoining the basilica, contains a whole range of objects devoted to the cult of St. Anne.

If the Carnac area enjoys a gentle climate and calm shores, it's thanks to the **Quiberon Peninsula,** a narrow, tapering strip of land bravely lunging out into the Atlantic. When you see the treatment the sea metes out to its west coast, its "wild" coast (Côte Sauvage), you realize how lucky Carnac is. Quiberon was an island that tide and wind attached to the mainland by forming a sandy, pebbly isthmus, at its narrowest just wide enough for the road and the railway to get by—with nothing to spare. Beaches on the protected east are pleasant and sandy while the **Côte Sauvage** on the west offers some of the most spectacular seascapes in Brittany. The Atlantic vents its fury on the jagged rocky seaboard. A coast road hugs the shoreline closely for some 12 kilometres from PORTIVY. You'll want to follow the footpaths past all the tiny uninhabited bays. Notices all along warn of the dangers of the deceptively calm creeks—and of those who gave their lives saving the imprudent.

Quiberon town itself is an agreeable resort at the tip of the peninsula, strong on thalassotherapy. The main beach arcs round just below, parallelled by an exceptionally animated waterfront promenade. Boats for **Belle-Ile,** the justly named "beautiful island" less than an hour away, leave from Quiberon's Port-Maria—well worth a day's outing if you have time. From **Le Palais,** you can rent a bicycle or a car, or as most people do, take the *car* (coach), whose tours coincide with boat arrivals and departures, for a round of the island with miles of varied, luxuriant scenery and dramatic coastline.

Vannes

Capital of the Morbihan *département,* Vannes is a provincial town in the best sense of the word: its old walled centre, hedged by the ramparts on one side, with the Gare Maritime to the south at the start of the canal, is on a human, even toy-like scale.

A good place to start a sightseeing tour is up at the **cathedral.** If you arrive by car, leave it in the Hôtel de Ville (Town Hall) parking place. Cars are out—you'll see why wandering around the narrow old streets. The building itself may have no great artistic merit—it's rather a mixture of styles from 13th to 19th centuries—but the **Chapelle du Saint-Sacrement,** decorated outside with scallop shells, is pure Italian Renaissance, a rare sight in Brittany. In the former chapterhouse of 1782, the **treasury** displays quite exceptional religious objects.

Just beside the cathedral is the so-called **Cohue,** a "medieval" covered market. Artisans in a bubble of activity and bustle sell their crafts and wares, not all of which are to be disdained. The Place Henri-IV and the charming little streets all around with timber houses at cockeyed angles merit investigation, Rue Noë in particular, site of the **Musée Archéologique** housed in the 15th-century Château-Gaillard. This important museum contains many of the prehistoric items found during excavations at Carnac, Locmariaquer and on the Rhuys Peninsula.

Vannes' medieval side is further accentuated in the evening when the ramparts (13th–17th centuries) are lit up and the walls come to life, with the cathedral in the background

and magnificent gardens *à la française* directly below. At one corner of the ramparts facing the Promenade de la Garenne lies the famous **lavoir** (washing place) whose delightful roof and setting has provided many a film with a medieval decor.

Gulf of Morbihan

The Bono and Auray rivers empty into the broad Gulf of Morbihan, best visited by boat. Some 50 islands (more or less, depending on the tides) lie scattered through a gulf 12 miles across, with an opening half a mile wide between Locmariaquer and Port-Navalo. Only 40 islands are actually inhabited (not all have electricity either), but the clement climate, lush Mediterranean vegetation, the effects of light, the changes at high and low tide and the sunsets form a superb whole. Add to this the long mud flats, oyster beds, fishermen, thatched or stone houses, and you have a fascinating world apart—memorable.

Regular launches *(vedettes vertes)* out into the gulf leave from Quai de la Rabine (several kilometres outside Vannes proper). You can make a trip to Ile d'Arz, Ile-aux-Moines, Port-Navalo and Locmariaquer or various combinations of the above. The complete round takes two hours, but a day's not too much to spend if you stop en route.

The little **Ile d'Arz** lives mostly from oyster culture, sheep farming and agriculture. The **Ile aux Moines** is not only the biggest island, it's also the most picturesque. As you land, you'll immediately fall for the lovely if tiny capital of the island, **Locmiquel.** Stroll up through the narrow streets, with painted white houses and flowers galore. If the balmy climate attracts many, the beaches, the lovely pinewoods and isolation bring even more.

Of all the megalithic monuments in Brittany, the minute island of **Gavrinis** has by far the most interesting specimen: a cairn 26 feet high and 328 feet in circumference. A long gallery flanked by stone slabs decorated all over with neat squiggles, signs and drawings, leads to the funeral chamber topped by a great, flat single stone (13 by 10 ft.). Excavations continue around this enigmatic site, thought to be 4,000 years old. The cairn is lighted by wind-generated electricity; if it fades, it's nothing to do with Breton creatures of legend. The normal boat trip goes, tantalizingly, beside it; to visit, take the launch from Larmor-Baden, a ten-minute trip. **71**

At one point, you'll head out of the gulf through the narrow channel into the ocean, where the current tugs and the boat seems frighteningly frail...

You can, of course, also drive a zigzag course round the gulf. Start perhaps from Auray, to take in its lovely river, continuing past **Bono,** a charming little port. All the way along you have delightful vistas of the river. Passing BADEN you reach the small port of LARMOR-BADEN, from where the boat leaves for the island of Gavrinis. The road continues to PORT-BLANC (regular launch for Ile aux Moines).

On the other side of the River Auray, towards the mouth of the gulf, the charming village of **Locmariaquer** has other claims to fame than its superb oysters. Head into the village and take the path marked "Table des Marchands". In a clearing, smashed into four massive blocks, lies what must have been the biggest menhir standing, dwarfing the humans that put it there.

Further along is the **Table des Marchands** itself, a tumulus covered by a vast slab of rock forming a "table top". If it has been raining, the corridor becomes rapidly muddy as crowds parade through it, studying the indecipherable jottings inside.

Like a pair of claws, the Rhuys Peninsula and the Pointe de Kerpenhir extend their pincers from opposite ends of the mainland and clutch in the Gulf of Morbihan with its archipelago.

Palms, fig trees and exotic plants flourish on the **Rhuys Peninsula,** protected from the worst of the winds by the Quiberon Peninsula. Seawater used to fill the moat of the massive 13th-16th century castle of **Suscinio;** dismantled at the Revolution, its craggy ruins are now under serious restoration.

A few miles west, **Saint-Gildas-de-Rhuys** has an ancient history: Abelard (of Heloise and Abelard fame) spent ten years here as abbot of the cloister. He had little good to say about the abbey, the country or the people, especially as they were trying to poison him. Faced with a monks' revolt, he fled in 1132, but the monastery buildings founded by St. Gildas in the 6th century still stand, totally restored in the 18th century, and serve as a rest-home. Certain parts of the neighbouring **abbey church,** however, date from Abelard's time: the choir with fine capitals and the transept are pure Romanesque. Tombstones from the 11th to 18th centuries line the walls, while behind the altar the grave of St. Gildas lies below a simple slab. A superb collection of reliquaries and cult objects such as the mitre of St. Gildas are well presented in the **treasury.**

On the way to lovely port-cum-resort of PORT-NAVALO, the **Tumulus de Tumiac** (also called Butte de César) affords superb views. Caesar is said to have stood here watching while his fleet scattered and decimated that of the Veneti—the Celtic tribe that valiantly tried to take him on.

Marshes and Peninsulas

Between the estuaries of the Vilaine and the Loire lie two distinct, self-contained areas: the Guérande Peninsula and the Grande Brière. The one boasts fashionable resorts backed by a salt marsh that hovers somewhere between sea and land; the other, La Grande Brière, is a world of its own, a mysterious canal-crossed marsh with traditions and a life-style apart.

The walls of **Guérande** are virtually intact; so is its charm. The main town entrance gate, the handsome Porte Saint-Michel, serves as the premises of the **Folklore Museum,** giving a fascinating overall view of the life, customs and costumes, furniture and professions of the area. The functioning of the salt industry, centred on the *marais salants* (salt marshes) to the west, can be followed thanks to a plan.

Guérande goes in for artisans and craftsmen and its main street, the animated Rue Saint-Michel, flows over with commerce of all types, while sinuous alleyways lead off towards the walls. Right in the centre of town stands the massive **Collégiale Saint-Aubin.** The colossal pillars and their circular capitals bear witness to the Romanesque origins of the church.

The contrasts—striking and total—of the **Guérande Peninsula** itself begin even as you leave its "capital". The Bois d'Amour is not an estate agent's catchy name for a housing estate, but a real wood planted in the 19th century to hold down the sand dunes. (The name has also been given to the coast here—Côte d'Amour.)

Today the wood lies behind the chic waterfront of **La Baule,** called—arguably not without reason—the most beautiful beach in Europe. Its five miles of fine sand, sprinkled with beach and sailing clubs, stretches in a perfect half-moon as far as the eye can see. The broad, tree-lined **boulevard** with its seafront walkways, the elegance of the façades and the lush vegetation have shades of Cannes, but there's no mistaking this as Brittany—albeit a particularly mild, sun-blessed region of Brittany. At either end, PORNICHET and LE POULIGUEN continue the resort with superb pleasure boat facilities.

Towards Le Croisic, outside the Bay of La Baule, the coast becomes progressively wilder and more open. Dark seaweed clings to the rocks and the Breton-style houses are set on patches of moorland.

Batz-sur-Mer (pronounced Bah) fronts onto the sea. The square, unmistakable 17th-century tower of the church of **Saint-Guénolé**—visible for miles around—offers a grandiose if windy view of contrasts. Before you lies the sea in all its majesty; behind, the strange, silent world of the *marais salants,* with its honeycomb of subtle greens, yellows, browns, blues and blotches of white. Occasional roads snake their way through the watery patchwork. In the distance you can make out the walls of Guérande. Below, at your feet, spread the Gothic ruins of the chapel of **Notre-Dame-du-Mûrier.**

Le Croisic is a pleasant holiday town which turned from sardine fishing to oyster-breeding, shellfish—and tourism. The beaches lie just outside

town. The harbour exudes charm—its small, low fishermen's houses still as they always were, the boats being repaired and repainted in the dock below.

This vast expanse of marshland, the **Marais Salants,** is fed with salt water from the tongue of sea penetrating in at high tide from Le Croisic. The salt pans occupy some 5,000 acres. The sea water is brought up to them via canals and left to decant in increasingly shallow basins, until it reaches the so-called *œillets* (literally, "eyelets") a mere two inches deep, where the salt crystallizes.

Although times are hard and salt has proved easier to obtain in warmer climes, where drying it out is less difficult, in its day Guérande's salt industry flourished and its people grew rich as salt was exchanged for cereals.

Centre of the salt area is SAILLÉ built on a former island where 27-pound sacks of salt are stacked for sale beside every house. A **museum,** the Maison des Paludiers, illustrates the life of the marsh workers, displaying engravings, work tools, furniture and costumes, plus a slide show.

Tidy bathing huts ring the long and elegant beach at La Baule.

To get a full view of the area and its industry penetrate in amid the *œillets* and head for Sissables, an isolated hamlet in the very centre of the marshland.

East of Guérande begins **La Grande Brière**, a remote and strange marsh area where man lives in perfect but fragile harmony with nature—and where sky, water and earth achieve a precarious ecological balance. Twenty-one *communes* (villages) make up this nature park of 100,000 acres, of which 17,500 are covered by marsh. More than 60 miles of canals called *chalandières* crisscross the marsh. No road cuts across the marsh: take a guided tour in a *chaland* (punt) from **Ile de Fédrun,** and spend an hour gliding around this extraordinary region. Once on the canals you will be in the kingdom of reeds and rushes. You will watch eels flee, carp jump, pike dance in the heavy waters of the marsh, with the pervasive smell of dank water all around and complete silence beyond the movement of the boat and the flight and cries of wild ducks, teal and snipe.

Guérande sea salt—guaranteed pure.

Central Brittany

Less known, less visited and by the same token more genuine, the interior or Argoat (Land of Woods), as it's called, cannot claim the drama or grandeur of the coast, but has plenty to offer. It's big, often sparsely populated and varied, ranging from the lowlands, a region of valleys and rivers, to hilly, even mountainous districts.

Geologically, quite some millions of years ago, the area of the Monts d'Arrée and the Montagnes Noires resembled the Alps. Erosion reduced the lofty peaks to hills. Even so, their desolation and barren isolation give them a noble, even grand, air.

Uplands

Hang-gliders leap off the **Ménez-Hom** (1,085 feet), tallest peak in the coastal area (see p. 52). Visible from many different spots along the coast it looms up from afar, a monk's tonsured head with a green rim of lush vegetation. The view from the peak is pretty stunning on all sides, extending from Brest and Pointe de Saint-Mathieu, past the Crozon Peninsula to the Bay of Douarnenez, while the Montagnes Noires stretch away inland.

Châteaulin lives from 77

salmon: salmon figures on its coat-of-arms, salmon figures on its menus and salmon teem in the River Aulne that meanders through it. A gentle calm pervades the little town and its shady quaysides, with green hills behind.

The Aulne meanders on through lovely scenery towards CHÂTEAUNEUF-DU-FAOU, but the road takes a straighter course to **Pleyben**. The town is famous for its *galettes* (biscuits or cookies) and its parish close —one of the finest and oldest examples in Brittany. The **calvary** (restored 1650), by its sheer volume, must be the province's biggest, and the ossuary, partly hidden by beautiful cedars, one of the oldest (1550). But it's the two **church towers** that give the hill town its particular look: from miles away they're clearly visible.

Brasparts, to the north-east, leads a lonely existence in a superb landscape, its parish close a small, perfect example of the art. You're now in the highest area of Brittany, the desolate Monts d'Arrée. The mists come down and render the atmosphere yet more sinister: not surprisingly the Bretons placed the entry to hell around here.

If **Huelgoat** is a pretty little town in its own right, it's the forest around it, and more specifically the stories and the legends surrounding them, that make a stop here not to be missed. As swans drift across the faintly melancholic "lake", skiffs flit over the waters and fishermen sit peacefully in their boats. At the top end of the lake begins a series of walks through Arthurian legend-land. For here amid a fantastic rocky chaos—in the remains of the vast forest that covered virtually the whole of Brittany's interior—come to life the legends of Brocéliande (see p. 80). Follow the map routes, and visit such rocky sights as the Chaos du Moulin and the swivelling Roche Tremblante.

Only a few miles further west, the jagged **Roch Trévezel** beside **Commana** (visit the parish close) provides more desolate views. Over 160,000 acres of mountainous terrain has been turned into a nature park, the **Parc Régional d'Armorique,** with administrative headquarters and a visitors' information bureau at the Domaine de Ménez-Meur near HANVEC. Within the confines of the park are various agricultural hamlets and animal sanctuaries. The little village of SAINT-RIVOAL has an open-air *écomusée,* showing former farming techniques and traditions.

Lowlands

If the mountain areas have much of the drama, they do not by any means monopolize the beauty spots or the artistic and historic treasures of inland Brittany.

The charming little town of **Le Faouët**, 20 kilometres north of Quimperlé, is a case in point. Its huge covered market *(La Cohue)* of 1542 remains a focus for community life, while around the town, close by, and amid extremely picturesque gentle countryside, lie three astonishing **chapels: the Chapelle Sainte-Barbe** with its beautiful Renaissance staircase; the Gothic **Chapelle Saint-Nicolas**, noted for the lovely Renaissance rood screen; and **Chapelle Saint-Fiacre**, remarkable for the vivid carved decoration of the fabulous wooden spandrels and rood screen, executed by a certain Olivier Loergan in 1480, the same date as the Gothic chapel.

Construction of **Kernascléden**'s church (1453), to the east, was financed by the Rohan viscounts and by Jean V, Duke of Brittany, and Jeanne de France, his wife. The volume of their combined contributions can be gauged in the wealth of sculptural detail on the porches—particularly the larger one to the left, where polychrome apostles stand proudly in their niches. Fine tracery, a thin spire, foliated pinnacles and carvings combine to give the church a light feel.

Contrary to most Breton churches, the vaults of Kernascléden are of stone, not wood. And that's not the only difference. These vaults and the walls beneath boast one of the oldest and best collections of 15th-century **wall paintings** in France. In the choir 24 scenes depict the life of the Virgin Mary and the childhood of Christ, while in the southern arm of the transept, scenes of hell, horror and torture send shivers down your spine.

Napoleon, in a handsome gesture to a loyal town, chose **Pontivy**—beside the River Blavet in the very middle of Brittany—as capital of the province and changed its name to Napoléonville. It was duly changed back afterwards, but not before considerable improvements had been made. When Pontivy fell back to sleep again, it had been transformed into a pleasant provincial community, with installations too big for its needs. Grouped round the old main square, Place du Martray, heart of the town, stand ancient houses, including the hunting lodge (1578) of the dukes of Rohan. **79**

Jean II de Rohan built Pontivy's sturdy **castle** in 1485.

A thick curtain of forest used to form a kind of natural frontier between Brittany and France. The needs of the navy and iron smelteries rapidly depleted the woods, till today a ring around Paimpont is about all that's left of the famous **Forêt de Paimpont,** better (and formerly) known as the Forêt de Brocéliande. Some 25 square miles remain—enough to get totally and utterly lost in, especially if you're following on the traces of Merlin, Vivian and the heroes of Arthurian legend.

Start at PAIMPONT, a little single-street *bourgade,* built around a former abbey with its medieval church and tranquil lake. The *Syndicat d'Initiative* in the abbey buildings distributes plans of possible walks through the woods. It makes the scene more living if you read up the tales of Chrétien de Troyes beforehand. You will want to go to such romantic spots as the Fontaine de Barenton, reached from the hamlet of Folle-Pensée; if you pour water on the Perron de Merlin beside it you'll bring a storm

Tour the chapels of central Brittany—or picnic in the woods.

down upon yourself. The oaks and beeches of old are being replaced by pines and fir trees, but the sense of mystery, the rays of sunlight filtering through the leaves, the smells, the silence, the myriad ponds, the paths hold good.

Josselin is part-fortress, part-château, part-feudal, part-Renaissance, depending on the side you approach from. It's imposing, charming and in a delightful village, with an interesting **basilica.**

The original castle was razed by the English in 1168, but up it went again in 1173, changing hands a number of times until in 1370 it reached Olivier de Clisson, a staunch partisan of the French cause in Brittany. On his death the château fell to the Rohan family—and to further tribulations: Duke François II of Brittany, Anne de Bretagne's father, had it dismantled in 1488 (the Rohans were too pro-French for his taste), but Anne, when she be-

came Queen of France, compensated Jean II de Rohan liberally and he in turn put up a masterpiece in the taste of the day.

Rising sheer from the river, the **château**'s curtain walls, battlements and turreted fortifications lead you to imagine a real fortress. From the other side, the surprise is total: you see a Renaissance masterpiece of a façade, with fretted pinnacles, decorative stonework balustrades and narrow gables, all in that granite so difficult to sculpt. Inside there are plenty of paintings, furniture, china and memorabilia, set in a lived-in context.

Although technically you should talk of the Forteresse de Largoët outside ELVEN, it's generally known as the **Tours d'Elven**, because all that remains of the castle is two towers. But what towers! Set in the middle of a park, down a long bumpy drive, they look like pieces in a chess set. The wind sweeps through the hollow, haunted shell, buried beneath ivy; the dungeon soars to 145 feet. Charles VIII of France, as he advanced to deliver the *coup de grâce* to the Breton cause, knocked down the château in 1488, as the Maréchal de Rieux had backed the "wrong" (Breton) side.

The Marches with France

Like a series of pickets, a row of châteaux on the border with France provided Brittany with a defensive shield against such a powerful neighbour. It also provided the route by which French culture later filtered into the province.

If châteaux are often built on rocky spurs, **Fougères** is an exception: the "new" town is on the hill above, while the 12th–15th century **castle** crouches below in its valley. Hugely powerful, virtually impregnable in the days before artillery, it stands at a strategic crossroads, once gripped within a loop of the River Nançon.

Study the layout from above, from the beautiful gardens of Place aux Arbres, before walking down along the ramparts to the gate at the Tour de la Haye-Saint-Hilaire. Once across the drawbridge, you're only in the Cour de l'Avancée; the castle proper lies through the Tour de Coëtlogon. From here you can walk round the ramparts and see various towers of the original 13, including the finest, Tour Mélusine.

Take the opportunity to visit the surprising **shoe museum** in Tour Raoul (Fougères was the

Formidable Fougères, a master-piece of military architecture, once defended Brittany's border.

capital of France's shoe indus-try till it fell on hard times). You should also pay a visit to the flamboyant Gothic **church** of Saint-Sulpice (you've already seen it from the ram-parts); its pointed belfry is remarkably elegant. Inside is a sculpture of Mélusine the Fairy, doing herself up before her mirror.

Next major link in the chain of châteaux is **Vitré**, dominant feature of the town of the same name, 29 kilometres south of

Fougères. This is the gateway to Brittany. No other town in the province has kept its me-dieval image so well as Vitré, with the possible exception of Dinan. Arriving from "France", you are inevitably struck by the distinctive ar- **83** chitecture, the deep-grey slate roofs and pepperpot towers, the granite and the haughty, graceful, triangular **castle** towering over the little town, formerly a rich sailcloth, hemp and cotton centre. The museum inside the château contains some interesting Breton furniture, among other items.

Barely a few yards beyond the château, **Rue Beaudrairie** retains the ambiance of times past. Each house, many of them 16th and 17th century, has character. The surrounding streets all contribute to the feel of a wealthy, bustling community, even today when the modest craftsmen of old have given way to souvenir artisans. Powerful ramparts encircle the town.

Mme. de Sévigné, a famous literary figure of the 17th century, came often to Vitré, the nearest town to her château of **Les Rochers,** 6½ kilometres away. Les Rochers belonged to her husband, a flighty Breton aristocrat, who managed to squander a fortune before getting himself killed in a duel seven years after their marriage. The 14th-century château (revamped in the 17th) has barely changed since Mme. de Sévigné's time. At the entrance stands the tiny chapel of 1671 (now the ticket office). Also on view is Mme. de Sévigné's

bedroom, the Cabinet Vert (Green Room), with various reminders of her life here. Mme. de Sévigné put her heart and soul into the planning of the garden. Laid out by Le Nôtre *à la française,* it is infinitely appealing.

In inland Brittany fewer traces of prehistoric presence are met with, so it is particularly welcome to come upon one of the highspots of megalithic architecture in a clearing beneath some venerable oak trees: **La Roche-aux-Fées** (The Fairies' Rock), south-west of Vitré. Forty-odd blocks of purple schist create a long chamber, those on top weighing between 40 and 45 tons. Just how many stones there are is a mystery: placed there by fairies, it's impossible to count their *exact* number . . .

Rennes

Capital of Brittany and archrival of Nantes, Rennes (population: 210,000) today is a university town with light and heavy industry and a busy,

Music has its own rewards in attractive medieval Rennes.

prosperous provincial air about it. The city had its beginning where the River Vilaine meets the Ille. While Nantes (now severed from Brittany and attached to the Loire region) served as capital of the old duchy of Brittany, the dukes were crowned at Rennes. The engagement between Anne of Brittany and Charles VIII was celebrated there. After union with France, Rennes became in 1561 the seat of Brittany's parliament. A fire in 1720 destroyed much of the medieval centre and the town suffered severe bombardments during the last war; but there's more than enough left to make a most interesting day.

The **old part** of Rennes, a small, easily walkable area, has kept a good number of 16th-century habitations—paunchy, cockeyed, wood-beamed and picturesque. Stroll through the tortuous streets surrounding the 19th-century Cathédrale Saint-Pierre and over to the Porte Mordelaise, the last remnants of the 15th-century ramparts. Look into Place des Lices, now the meat market, where jousting once took place. Wander through the area around Place du Champ Jaquet for more medieval ensembles, then head across to the more classical and formal Law Courts

and the straight streets around them.

This district was restructured in the 18th century after designs elaborated by the architects Jacques Gabriel and his son Jacques-Ange, with a grid street plan and standardized (and fireproof) stone structures. In Place du Palais, a French-style garden faces the **Palais de Justice** (Law Courts). Begun in 1618, the austere yet noble edifice is richly decorated within. Guided tours visit the Grande-Chambre, formerly the meeting place of the Breton Parliament, the impressive Salle des Assises with its elaborate woodwork and the vast barrel-vaulted Salle des Pas-Perdus.

Pride of the **Hôtel de Ville** (Town Hall), designed by Jacques Gabriel, is the clock atop its tower; called "le Gros" (The Big One), it's the only surviving part of the old building.

One of the great museums of Brittany is undoubtedly Rennes' **Musée de Bretagne** across the River Vilaine. Exhibits trace

Brittany is for children: junior gymnasts line up at Perros-Guirec.

the history of the Bretons and the unnamed, little-known peoples who were here before them. In addition, examples of Breton furniture, costumes and documents are presented logically and clearly. Problems of today are not eluded, and films show unusual and interesting aspects of Brittany.

The upper floors house a **fine arts museum** *(Musée des Beaux Arts),* with a superb collection of European art, including ancient and modern masters.

What to Do

In the realm of activities, Brittany has more than enough to satisfy participants and spectators, with never a dull moment.

Sports

It's obviously in the area of water sports that Brittany has the most to offer, though it's far from the whole story.

Water Sports

Generalizing, north Brittany offers stronger currents, bigger tides (differences of up to 50 feet sometimes), more dramatic rock formations. South Brittany can propose easier, more relaxed sailing, more sophisticated facilities and more sun.

Swimming. Good beaches are to be found around La Baule and the Gulf of Morbihan, in the Bénodet area (Loctudy, Beg-Meil), around the "prongs" of Cornouaille and along the Côte de Granit Rose and the Emerald Coast. The choice of beach ranges from the long, fine-sand variety to the dune type (Presqu'île de Sainte-Marguerite, Pointe du Grouin) and more intimate coves. Facilities, comfort, waves, scenery and activities vary considerably from area to area.

Water-skiing. Most resorts have a wide channel at right-angles to the coast where boats can beach at a speed of 5 knots. Out in the open, you can scud along to your heart's content—but be safety-conscious. In the main resort centres boats and equipment are readily available for hire.

Spear-fishing and Underwater Diving. No one pretends the seas are as warm as those of the Mediterranean, and the tides, currents and undercur-

rents can complicate a diver's movements. However, the Breton continental shelf offers sensations and sights like nowhere else: exceptionally rich sea life, as well as several underwater archaeological sites, like Er Lanic in the Gulf of Morbihan.

Unless you are a member of a club affiliated with the French Federation of Underwater Sports, it is obligatory to contact the portside authorities *(Bureau des Affaires Mari-*

times) before you take the plunge. It is forbidden to fish with compressed-air tanks, or even to have any in your boat. Keep clear of waters where diving and fishing are prohibited and take only what is permitted: fish and crustaceans to a maximum of six per person per day, outside breeding areas. For your own safety, don't approach within 165 yards of fishing boats or nets.

Boardsailing / Windsurfing. Even if you're not alone (and

Futuristic buildings of La Baule echo the sweep of the beach.

you *can* be if you start early), there's room for everyone. Keep out of the way of bathers in their fenced-off areas, but don't stray further than one nautical mile from the shore. All equipment is on hire at major and many minor beaches, and plenty of schools provide instruction.

Boating. Brittany is about as **89**

good a spot as you can imagine for sailing. The wind blows with dependable regularity and usually gives fair warning when a storm is brewing. Breton coves, roadsteads, creeks and sheltered estuaries provide the less experienced with calm waters for smooth sailing. Each major port has a sailing school, and there are lakeside schools inland. The minimum age for most schools is eight (some go down to six).

There's plenty of fun, exploration and adventure on Brittany's rivers. Various schools give would-be canoeists instruction in descent and slalom. Request the indispensable guide to navigable rivers from the Ligue Régionale de Canoë-kayak, Rue du Grand-Martin, 35760-Saint-Grégoire.

Fishing. Brittany's canals and rivers teem with shad, eel, salmon and many other species. Anglers will find every type of fishing imaginable, much of it original and unusual because of the meeting of marsh, river and sea. Along the coast it's perfectly possible to join a deep-sea expedition, usually advertised down at the port, or to rent a dinghy and fish offshore. A *permis* may be required for other boats.

For further information on sea fishing, contact the Comité Régional de Bretagne-Vendée, Pont Roux, Le Yaudet, 22300 Ploumilliau.

Other Sports

Golf. Brittany has its share of golf courses, both nine and 18 holes. Most striking, perhaps, are the greens of Dinard-Saint-Briac. Others scattered round the coast and inland include La Bretesche, La Forêt-Fouesnant, Sables d'Or-Fréhel, Saint-Cast-le-Guildo. Green fees are generally reasonable.

Horse-riding. Galloping over an empty beach or through the *lande* induces an extraordinary feeling of liberty and well-being. Dozens of clubs exist all over Brittany; sign up for an hour, a day or a week. You can also rent out a horse from the *haras* (stud-farm) at Lamballe or Hennebont. There are signposted tracks throughout the province—notably in the forests of the Argoat around Paimpont. Riding holidays with accommodation and meals are available.

Tennis. Week-long intensive courses for players of all levels are held along the coast (mainly in the south) at La Trinité, La Baule, Carnac. For less serious enthusiasts, there are plenty of municipal courts to be hired by the hour and certain hotels have their own.

Shopping

Brittany's main centres—Rennes, Brest, Saint-Brieuc, La Baule, Saint-Malo, Vannes and Lorient—have all the best of France in their stores, in addition to a number of regional specialities. The French as a whole tend to be demanding shoppers: out to get the best at the best price, prepared to pay for quality but intransigent with the slipshod, keen on design and presentation.

Shopping Hours

Most shops and department stores open from 8 or 9 a.m. to noon and from 2 to 7 p.m., Tuesday to Saturday (many stores close on Mondays). But hours can be casual. In the summer, small establishments often close for longer periods in the middle of the day, but stay open later in the evening for the tourist trade. They may also open on Sundays.

What to Look For

Antiques. Shops throughout the province specialize in Breton peasant objects, such as farm instruments or old irons.

Ceramics. Earthenware bowls, plates, dishes can be found everywhere, inexpensively. Quimper-style pottery flooded the market for many years. It's manufactured in various forms, from oil-and-vinegar dispensers to dinner sets. Best selection in Quimper itself (see p. 61).

Cider. More heady than one might think, and fitting for many an occasion, *cidre* makes an inexpensive present. The best comes from Fouesnant.

Clogs. Genuine handmade *sabots* (still worn by a few local people) can be purchased in small villages like Batz-sur-Mer.

Coats. Traditional *kabigs,* similar to duffle coats, keep winter winds at bay. *Cabans* (reefers) and *cirés* (oilskins) can be useful here—or at home.

Dolls. Beautiful, dressed up in the costumes of Pont-l'Abbé, Quimper, Pont-Aven, etc.

Furniture. Brittany is one of Europe's last bastions of handmade furniture (Lannion, Batz-sur-Mer, Morbihan in particular). If you can't transport a hand-turned cupboard, you might manage a stool. Often good value.

Galettes. In tins, boxes or packets, sweet biscuits (cookies) from Pont-Aven or Pleyben always make welcome presents—if you can part with them.

Jerseys. The Bretons wear 91

hardy, hand-knitted wool pull-overs *(chandail breton)* in solid colours or stripes. Practical, perfect for the climate, they come in adults' and children's sizes, with scarves and berets to match.

Jewellery. Plenty of tasteful designs available, often with Celtic motifs.

Lace. Many people appreciate the hand-made lace *(dentelle)* of Brittany—a tradition kept alive by the tourist trade. Pont-l'Abbé, Quimper and Rennes are the places to buy lace.

Metalware. Objects of wrought iron, bronze and pewter—from gates to lampstands and ashtrays—are a Breton speciality, available mainly in Lannion, Rennes, Vitré, Quimper.

Nautical goods. Well-conceived, practical, or simply decorative supplies for all kinds of vessels, from yachts to liners.

Shells, driftwood, minerals. Collect your own or buy typical specimens (Le Croisic) or ornaments incorporating these materials (Quiberon, Camaret).

Stone carving. Artisans sculpt granite into everything from elves to amphoras.

Wickerwork. In the Brière region, artisan families have been making baskets and other items for centuries.

Entertainment

Late in the evening, crowds gather along the sea front (wrapped up against the wind) and have a coffee on the beach-side terraces. The more energetic move on to nightclubs and discotheques—some of which are housed in converted barns in the countryside—or to the casinos of Dinard, Sables-d'Or-les-Pins, La Baule and Perros-Guirec.

If you have a chance, attend a typical *fest noz* (literally, "night festival"), a get-together that takes all forms from games, competitions and athletics to dancing cheek-to-cheek. The local *Syndicat d'Initiative* will provide you with information.

Sound-and-light shows in various historic localities provide a memorable evening's entertainment (e.g. at the Tours d'Elven). Rennes and Nantes offer theatres and, occasionally, opera possibilities. The cinemas outside the main centres may not have the most up-to-date films, and many, if not most, foreign films are dubbed into French.

Quimper's decorative pottery is a high street attraction.

Pardons

The religious fervour of the Bretons has kept the pardons alive longer in Brittany than elsewhere. The ceremony—mass or vespers with a procession either before or after—is followed by a general rejoicing afterwards.

The pardon originated as a kind of mass pilgrimage; the Church, on the Feast of the Assumption and on saints' days, granted a pardon (plenary indulgence) to repentant sinners participating in the ceremony. Particular pardons are dedicated to patron saints credited with healing virtues, great or small, the Virgin Mary and Ste. Anne, for example. But many have never been recognized by the Church. Credited with powers to heal physical ailments but also able to minister to the soul, Brittany's unofficial saints are the original 6th-century Breton religious leaders who came from Wales, Cornwall or Ireland.

Pardons are held all over Brittany, in every village, commune or hamlet, and the colour and fervour are most moving. Most famous are the following: *Rumengol:* Trinity Sunday; *Sainte-Anne-la-Palud:* the Sunday after August 18th; *Sainte-Anne-d'Auray:* July 26th; *Le Folgoët:* first Sunday in September.

Folklore and Festivals

It's impressive, the number of summer events in Brittany. The emphasis is on cultural festivals (art exhibitions, concerts, classical dance, theatre) and folklore manifestations. Following are the major events of general interest and amusement from April to October:

Festival des Arts Traditionnels, Rennes. At the end of *April,* Breton dances, music and costume take centre stage.

Concours de Musique Gallère, Monterfil. Upper Brittany's popular *June* music festival.

Festival de Brocéliande, Paimpont. Arthurian legend provides the theme for this *June* event.

Fête des Fraises, Plougastel. The strawberry harvest is cause for celebration on the third Sunday in *June.*

Les Tombées de la Nuit, Rennes. This arts festival held in early *July* celebrates Breton creativity.

Championnat de Lutte celtique, Belle-Ile-en-Terre. Contenders for the Celtic wrestling title fight it out on the third Sunday in *July.*

Festival de Danses bretonnes, Guingamp. Traditional dances are the prime attraction of this *July* festival.

Young and old participate enthusiastically in ritual of the pardon.

Fête des Pommiers, Fouesnant. Watch for *coiffes* at this popular gathering on the third Sunday in *July.*

Grandes Fêtes de Cornouaille, Quimper. Late in *July,* citizens of Cornwall's capital don traditional dress and make merry.

Festival Théâtre et Danse, Hédé. A big event in a little village, the festival of theatre and dance attracts people from all over in early *August.*

Festival Interceltique, Lorient. This international gathering of Celtic (Breton, Welsh, Irish, Scottish) groups takes place in early *August.*

Fête des Fleurs d'Ajoncs d'Or, Pont-Aven. Crowds throng Gauguin's village to celebrate the *August* blooming of the gorse.

Fête de la Jeunesse et de la Mer, Dinard. At the end of *Au-* **95** gust, this popular resort pays tribute to its seafaring traditions.

Grande Fête des Menhirs, Carnac. Brittany's "prehistoric capital" remembers its past on the third Sunday in *August.*

Fête des Filets Bleus, Concarneau. Costumes, processions and folk events are the highlight of the *August* "Blue Nets" festival in honour of sardine fishermen.

Bogue d'Or, Redon. *October* competition of stories, songs and traditional music.

Bagpipes are Breton, too.

Eating Out

Happily, eating out in Brittany is like eating out anywhere in France, with a plus—the seafood. Although the province doesn't enjoy a great reputation within France for original and great cuisine, you'll return home with glorious memories of good food.

Where to Eat

Brittany has restaurants of all kinds, from simple family-run eating houses to luxury establishments serving French *haute cuisine*. The many *crêperies*, snack bars and outdoor food-vending carts cater to holiday-makers in a hurry or on a budget.

Breakfast

In Brittany, as elsewhere in France, breakfast tends to be summary but delicious: croissants, bread and butter with a mug of good coffee, a pot of tea or cup of chocolate. You might obtain an English-style breakfast in the larger seaside resorts if you ask for it.

Lunch

In the French hierarchy, lunch is important. But many people find it daunting to undertake two gargantuan meals a day. A picnic in the countryside or on a rocky headland makes a pleasant alternative.

Charcuteries or *traiteurs* (caterers) pack cooked meat and fresh salads to take away. The *boulangerie* provides bread —typical long *baguette*, *pain de campagne* and wholemeal *pain complet*—and the *pâtisserie* sells sweets—*éclairs*, *religieuses* and *mille-feuilles,* local specialities rich with eggs, sugar and butter. Don't forget a bottle of cider (*cidre*—buy it *"brut"* if you like it dry) or some rosé or white wine.

If the weather doesn't permit a picnic, another quick and inexpensive solution is the ubiquitous Breton *crêperie,* where you can eat as much or little as you like. You could start with a *crêpe (au froment) au beurre* (buckwheat pancake with butter) or *au fromage* (with cheese), and perhaps go on to a seafood or meat *crêpe*—and if you're still hungry, have a sweet *crêpe* dessert.

For those who feel the urge for tea, certain *pâtisseries* double as tea-rooms.

Dinner

The gastronomic highlight of the day is, of course, dinner; after sightseeing or strenuous sports come the pleasures of the table. While you'll find the seafood superb, the province also offers a wide selection of good French dishes that are more or less common to restaurants all over the country.

Starters

Most menus list familiar and delicious starters: tomatoes and cucumbers in season, *céleri remoulade* (shredded celeriac in mustard-mayonnaise dressing) and an array of terrines, *charcuterie* or *crudités* (mixed salads). If you see more specifically Breton items (e.g. *sardines grillées, maquereaux,* mackerel or *langoustines,* prawns) try them.

Fish and shellfish are so important to a Breton meal that we treat them at length below. Another speciality is pork, and first courses may include several types of pork pâté and sausage. *Rillettes* means potted pork, soft enough to spread like a pâté on bread.

Meat and Vegetables

Besides fish, the Bretons—like most of their countrymen—relish meat. The speciality here, shared with neighbouring Normandy, is undoubtedly *gigot d'agneau pré-salé* (leg of lamb from animals raised in salt-saturated fields; the French like it medium rare); lamb may also be served as saddle *(selle),* rack

The World of the Oyster

In Brittany, oysters can be eaten all year round. The comma-shaped ones in rough, ruffled greyish shells *(creuses)* are broadly classified as *Portugaises*; they're usually cultivated these days, rather than wild, and have a very salty taste. The consistency can be fatty. You'll often see them listed as *fines de claire* (which denotes the type of pen they're raised in, called *clairière*) and *spéciales,* a type of *fines de claire.* Numbers after names on menus denote weight, going from 5 (lightest) to 1, 0 or even 000 (heaviest of all). Thus "fines de claires #2" would specify average-size Portuguaise oysters.

Belon and *Marenne* (from north of Royan) oysters have flat and comparatively smooth shells. Highly esteemed for their quality and a common type found in Brittany, they are less fatty and salty than Portugaises. Purists eat their oysters raw, with just a touch of lemon juice. But also ask for a sauce of red-wine vinegar and chopped shallots. Brown bread *(pain bis)* and butter make the best accompaniments.

(carré) or chops *(côtes).* The classic accompaniment for lamb is white beans; in fact, for any dish, the description *à la*

Oysters are at their freshest down by the port in Cancale.

Bretonne usually means "with white beans".

Bretons raise pigs, so naturally their pork roasts and chops can be excellent—plain or with various sauces. Here, too, you can sample *andouilles* and *andouillettes*—sausages made with variety meats—grilled and perhaps in sauce, usually with strong mustard. *Boudin* (blood sausage) is good with mustard and warm apple puree or mashed potatoes.

Excellent roast, poached or grilled chicken *(poulet)* is nearly always available, served plain, herbed or with various sauces: tarragon-cream *(à l'estragon)*, *suprême* (cream sauce), *diable* (spicy), *aux cèpes, aux morilles* (with bolet or morel mushrooms), and so on.

All types of beef are beloved all over France. Your *chateaubriand, filet* or equally good *faux-filet* may be ordered *bleu* (so rare it's practically on the hoof), *saignant* (rare), *à point* (medium) and *bien cuit* (well done).

The mild Breton climate makes it possible to find good fresh vegetables year-round. Artichokes, asparagus, green beans, cauliflower, Brussels **99** sprouts, carrots, peas, and of course, potatoes and rice, may appear with main courses, depending on the dish and season.

Fish and Shellfish

For starters, you might sample the *cotriade* (*kauteriad* in Breton), a hearty fish soup that's often compared to the *bouillabaisse* of Marseilles. The fishermen of old combined whole pieces of tunny fish, chunks of bread, potatoes and whatever else was going. Today it's a choice of sea bream, hake, conger eel, monkfish, mackerel, sardine, red mullet or John Dory. Fishheads are sometimes included. Or try one type of shellfish right out of the sea (such as a dozen oysters or some clams).

But the glory of Brittany is the gargantuan *plateau de fruits de mer,* an assortment of familiar and exotic-looking creatures arranged like a tableau on a bed of seaweed.

Apart from oysters, this cornucopia of seafood may include *palourdes* and *praires,* from the clam family, along with clams—perhaps the *rigadelle* type, the tiny *Vénus* or the *coque rayée.* You may be offered mussels *(moules),* scallops *(coquilles Saint-Jacques)* and Dublin Bay prawns *(langoustines),* as well as *bigor-* *neaux* (periwinkles), extracted from their shells with picks or pins. You'll also see *bulots* and *buccins* (whelks or sea snails), chewy *ormeaux* (ormers or abalone) and delicate-tasting *couteaux* (the shells look like razors).

Although the French prefer to eat their shellfish raw or cold, there are some delicious hot preparations. *Moules marinière* consists of mussels cooked in a white-wine broth, with onions or shallots, parsley and seasonings. Mussels are also delicious cooked in cider *(au cidre). Mouclade* is more refined: tiny mussels in a hot cream sauce with a touch of curry. *Coquilles Saint-Jacques* may be served in a saffron or a chive and butter sauce *(beurre blanc à la ciboulette)*—or in the classic *gratin* in cream sauce with mushrooms. Sometimes you'll see stuffed oysters or clams on menus *(huîtres/palourdes farcies),* delicious with herbs, breadcrumbs and a touch of garlic.

Lobster *(homard)* and the clawless spiny lobster *(langouste)* can be stuffed and

This glorious cornucopia of shellfish went straight from Breton waters to the table.

baked, boiled or grilled with melted butter or hollandaise sauce. *Homard à l'américaine* or *à l'armoricaine* is bathed in a rich sauce of tomato, cognac, shellfish stock, cream and much else.

Served whole in the shell, the many varieties of *crabe* prove to first-timers devilishly hard to eat, especially the very small *étrilles.* The *araignée de mer,* or spider crab, is esteemed for its succulent meat, while the *tourteau* has particularly delicate claw meat, roe in season and much else.

There's no shortage of fish to choose from. *Lotte* (a chewy kind of angler-fish that can taste like lobster), *limande* (lemon sole), *daurade* (sea bream) and *bar* (sea bass) are prepared in endless ways, with various sauces. *Beurre blanc Nantais* is a butter-based fish sauce invented and perfected in and around Nantes and the Loire Valley; delicate and yet slightly acidic with a touch of wine vinegar and chopped shallots, it turns a plain fish into a gourmet's delight.

Brittany is also known for its excellent fresh-water fish, mainly from the Loire, as it flows into the Atlantic. You may see fresh salmon *(saumon)* and pike *(brochet)* on the menu.

Dessert

Cheese is not a Breton speciality, but in your *plateau de fromages,* you'll probably have a good selection from all over, including some of the best from next-door Normandy.

But Brittany does have its share of mouth-watering sweets, besides the famed Breton dessert *crêpes* with honey, chocolate, fruit, jam and whipped cream garnishings.

Far Breton is a type of flan or custard cake, usually filled with a sprinkling of prunes or raisins, sometimes served in a crust. You may see *quatre-quarts,* a rich pound cake made with a fourth each of butter, flour, sugar and eggs. Don't try to pronounce it, but look for *Couign-aman,* a confection of buttery and sweet puff pastry that melts in the mouth.

Wine and Cider

Say "Breton wine" to any Frenchman, and he immediately thinks of *muscadet.* Indeed the region around Nantes produces a dry, fruity white wine that perfectly complements fish and shellfish. The main *appellations d'origine,* denoting where the wine is produced, are *Sèvre-et-Maine* and *Coteaux-de-la-Loire* and AOC (all other areas). On some bottles you will see *muscadet sur lie,* meaning that the wine has spent only one winter in a barrel and retained its sediment when bottled.

From towards Nantes' coastal region comes *gros-plant,* another white wine with a slightly lower alcohol content (11 degrees). The only local reds and rosés are *Coteaux-d'Ancenis-Gamay.*

Wines from elsewhere in France are available everywhere. Cider *(cidre),* often served by the cupful *(bolée)* makes an agreeable change: it is refreshing and packs a considerable punch.

To Help You Order...

Could we have a table?
Do you have a set menu?

Pouvons-nous avoir une table?
Avez-vous un menu du jour?

I'd like a/an/some...

Je désire...

butter	**du beurre**	milk	**du lait**
bread	**du pain**	mineral water	**de l'eau minérale**
chips	**des frites**		
coffee	**un café**	salt	**sel**
fish	**du poisson**	sugar	**du sucre**
fruit	**un fruit**	tea	**du thé**
ice-cream	**une glace**	(iced) water	**de l'eau (glacée)**
meat	**de la viande**		
menu	**la carte**	wine	**du vin**

...and Read the Menu

agneau	lamb	**fraises**	strawberries
ail	garlic	**framboises**	raspberries
artichauts	artichokes	**gigot**	leg
asperges	asparagus	**haricots verts**	string beans
bœuf	beef	**jambon**	ham
canard	duck	**melon**	melon
carottes	carrots	**moutarde**	mustard
chou	cabbage	**nouilles**	noodles
chou-fleur	cauliflower	**oignons**	onions
concombre	cucumber	**petits pois**	peas
côtelettes	chops, cutlets	**pommes**	apples
endive	chicory (endive)	**poulet**	chicken
		raisin	grapes
épinards	spinach	**saucisse/**	sausage
flageolets	beans	**saucisson**	

103

BLUEPRINT for a Perfect Trip

How to Get There

Because of the complexity and variability of the many fares, you should ask the advice of an informed travel agent well before your departure.

From Great Britain and Eire

Most visitors from the U.K. travel to Brittany individually, either by booking directly with a ferry operator and taking the car, or signing up for inclusive holidays which offer fly/drive and touring or self-catering arrangements.

BY AIR: Direct scheduled flights link London to Nantes, Rennes, Quimper and Morlaix. Service is increased during the summer season (end June to early September). Direct flights leave from Cork, Ireland, for Morlaix in the summer. Connecting flights by way of London or Paris serve many British provincial capitals.

You'll save money if you book a *PEX* or *SUPERPEX* fare, payable on booking, both of which require a minimum stay and carry an alteration or cancellation penalty. *Excursion* fares stipulate a minimum stay, but there are no other restrictions. Reductions are made for children.

BY SEA: There are regular car-ferry services (advance booking much recommended) from Great Britain to ports in Brittany (mainly Roscoff and Saint-Malo). Cherbourg, actually in Normandy, but convenient for Northern Brittany, is linked to Weymouth, Portsmouth, Poole and Rosslare (Ireland). Sleeping accommodation is available on night crossings. Look into the various packages on offer, combining transport and accommodation for stays of a couple of days to two weeks.

BY RAIL: Express trains operate from Paris to the principal towns and resorts in Brittany. Travel time averages between four and eight hours.

The *Inter-Rail Card* provides one month of unlimited second-class travel to those under 26. For old-age pensioners, the *RES (Rail Europ Senior) Card* is available to women over 60 and men over 65. Anyone permanently resident outside France can purchase the *Carte France Vacances* for specified periods of unlimited travel. Reductions are also made for families and groups (minimum 10 adults). Ask the French national tourist office for details.

From North America

BY AIR: A limited number of connecting flights (via Paris) link major cities in the United States and Canada to Brittany, but in general you should take one of the numerous direct flights from North America to Paris and arrange onward flights thereafter.

The main types of bargain fares available are *PEX, APEX, Youth Fares* and *Weekend Excursion Fares* (the latter available during certain parts of the year only). Consult a travel agent for the latest information about discounts and special deals.

When to Go

Brittany's "poor-weather" reputation (among Frenchmen) is unde-served. Summers are appreciably warmer than southern Britain and the Channel Islands. In winter, it rains frequently, but not all day. Snow and frost are infrequent and overall temperatures mild. Never-theless, summer or winter, be prepared for some wind (occasionally gale force!) and rain and for muddy country roads. Equally, however, don't forget your suntan lotion.

Temperatures in Southern Brittany (from about Quimper heading south) are noticeably higher and the sea water warmer. Here are some temperatures for Northern Brittany:

		J	F	M	A	M	J	J	A	S	O	N	D
average daily	°F	40	39	41	45	49	54	57	57	56	51	46	42
minimum*	°C	4	4	5	7	9	12	14	14	13	10	8	5
average daily	°F	47	47	51	54	59	64	67	67	65	60	53	49
maximum*	°C	8	8	10	12	15	18	19	20	19	15	12	10

Average hours of sunshine:
Summer   7–8
Winter   3–4

*Minimum temperatures are measured just before sunrise, maximum tempera-tures in the early afternoon.

Planning Your Budget

To give you an idea of what to expect, here is a list of average prices in french francs (F). They can only be *approximate,* however, as inflation in France, as elsewhere, creeps relentlessly up, and there are considerable regional and seasonal variations.

Baby-sitters. 30–50 F per hour, 150–200 F full day, Beach club 600 F a month (mornings 9 a.m.–12 noon).

Bicycle and moped hire. 40–55 F a day, deposit 200–250 F, moped 80–100 F, deposit 600 F.

Boat (motorized) **hire.** 150 F an hour, 400 F half-day, 600 F a day. Houseboats (8 people) weekend 2,475–3,000 F, week 6,300–7,500 F; (2 people) weekend 1,375 F, week 3,500 F.

Boat trips. Tour of Gulf of Morbihan 60 F; trip up Odet River (Bénodet–Quimper return) 60 F, Quiberon–Belle Ile 60 F, Arcouest–Bréhat 16 F, trip round Mont St. Michel Bay 65 F (children 40 F). Boat excursion from Douarnenez (1½ hours) 50 F. Deep-sea fishing excursion (4 hours) 100 F.

Camping. About 100 F for 2 persons per day including car and services, 12–25 F per extra person.

Car hire (international company). *Renault 5 GTL* 185 F per day, 2.30 F per km., 1,955 F per week with unlimited mileage. *Renault 11* 235 F per day, 3.20 F per km., 2,695 F per week with unlimited mileage. *BMW 520* 350 F per day, 4.20 F per km., 5,400 F per week with unlimited mileage. Taxes included.

Entertainment. Cinema 30–35 F, admission to discotheque 40–90 F, Sound and Light show (Elven) 45 F (children 20), cabaret 150–350 F.

Hairdressers. *Man's* haircut 70 F and up. *Woman's* haircut 80 F and up, blow-dry/shampoo and set 90 F and up, manicure 50 F and up.

Hotels (double room). ******** 600 F and up, ******* 300 F and up, ****** 200 F and up, ***** 150 F and up. *Youth hostels* 30–35 F per day.

Meals and drinks. Continental breakfast 15–50 F, crêpe meal 45 F with ¼ l. cider, lunch or dinner in fairly good establishment 75 F (120 F for superior menu, 200 F for gastronomic menu), dish of seafood and crustaceans 150 F, bottle of house wine 40 F, coffee 5 F, cognac 15–20 F.

Sports and sports equipment. Windsurf board 50 F an hour, 250 F a day (9 hours), tennis 55–80 F per hour, golf ca. 120 F (caddies 70 F, equipment 50 F).

An A–Z Summary of Practical Information and Facts

Listed after most main entries is an appropriate translation, usually in the singular. You'll find this vocabulary useful when asking for assistance.
For all prices, refer to list on page 107.

A

ACCOMMODATION (see also CAMPING). Brittany has long been a tourist magnet. Consequently it is well supplied with accommodation of all sorts, particularly in the family-orientated bracket. Only Rennes and Nantes—and Lorient, Brest, Dinard, La Baule, Carnac and Quiberon to a lesser extent—have international-style hotels.

Hotels. These are classed by the Direction du Tourisme in grades ranging from one- to four-star luxury establishments. Most hotels with their own restaurants expect you to take dinner when you stay the night. *Pension* (room and all meals) terms can usually be obtained for any stay of three days or over. *Demi-pension* (room, breakfast and evening meal) is usually available outside the peak holiday period.

Room prices, fixed according to amenities, size and the hotel's star rating, must be posted prominently at the reception desk and behind each room door. Hotels marked NN *(Nouvelles Normes)* have been reclassified and correspond to current standards of comfort.

If you're touring round in the holiday season, try and start looking for your hotel not later than 6 p.m.

Note: *hôtel de ville* is not a hotel, but the town hall.

Châteaux-Hôtels de France. These converted châteaux, covering the whole of France, are an expensive but worthwhile romantic alternative. They are listed together with **Relais de Campagne,** a similar chain offering a wider variety of hotels in country settings; rating from two to four stars. Some are genuine, old-time stagecoach inns. The book is available from tourist offices.

Logis de France, Auberges de France. Small or quiet hotels, often on the outskirts or outside of towns. *Logis de France* are in the one- and two-star bracket; *auberges de France* are typical inn-type establishments in the country. A *Guide des Logis de France* is produced annually and given out free at national tourist offices abroad. A very handy booklet, *Hôtels Logis et Auberges de Bretagne,* is also obtainable.

Gîtes de France, Gîtes Ruraux. Furnished holiday accommodation, **A** with standards and prices officially controlled. Your *gîte* could be a delightful surprise: a small cottage, a village house, a flat in the owner's house or part of a farm. Rental costs are inclusive of all charges.

Auberges de Jeunesse (youth hostels). Your national youth hostel association can give you all the details, or contact the Fédération Unie des Auberges de Jeunesse:

6, rue Mesnil, 75116 Paris; tel. 16~(1) 42.61.84.03.

Syndicats d'Initiative (see TOURIST INFORMATION OFFICES) throughout Brittany have their own additional lists of local accommodation.

a double/single room	**une chambre à deux lits/ à un lit**
with bath/shower/lavatory	**avec bains/douche/toilettes**
What's the rate per night?	**Quel est le prix pour une nuit?**

AIRPORTS. Brittany once suffered from its isolation. No longer. Quimper, Rennes, Dinard, Nantes, Saint-Brieuc, Morlaix, Lannion and Brest all have airports. These provide the necessary services with a minimum of formalities and fuss, and are usually not very far out of the town centres. Taxi planes are available at Brest, Nantes, Vannes, Lorient and Quiberon. The islands (apart from Ouessant) have no regular air connection. The two major airports serving Brittany are, for the southern areas, at Nantes (Château-Bougon, 10 km. south-west of the city) and for the northern, Saint-Malo/Dinard (Pleurtuit, 7 km. south of town).

BABY-SITTERS (see also CHILDREN). Hotels at seaside resorts usu- **B** ally can arrange for a sitter, at least someone to "look in". Alternatively, inquire at the *Syndicat d'Initiative* or check notice boards in supermarkets. Some clubs organize daytime activities.

Can you get me a baby-sitter for tonight?	**Pouvez-vous me trouver une garde d'enfants pour ce soir?**

BEACHES and SWIMMING. Swimming presents certain hazards. Breton waters are, after all, fairly cold, and currents can be strong. Some places (occasionally marked) have to be avoided purely and simply as too dangerous. Even though there are lifeguards on all main beaches, and safety is well enforced under their vigilant eye, prudence is necessary.

B

Look at the flags on the main beaches—they indicate whether it's safe (green) or too dangerous (red). If a beach is unguarded, ask first—it's only sensible to do so.

Can we swim here?   **Peut-on se baigner ici?**

BICYCLE and MOPED HIRE (location de bicyclettes/vélomoteurs). It's no problem to hire a bike: most of the main railway stations rent them out, by the day or week, with the possibility of returning them at another station. Otherwise, bicycle and moped shops are plentiful even in small towns and on the islands—where cars are few and far between (Belle-Ile) or illegal (Bréhat).

All moped and motorcycle riders (and their passengers) must wear crash helmets. Use of dipped headlights is obligatory at all times of day. Mopeds are forbidden on motorways.

I'd like to hire a bicycle/moped.   **Je voudrais louer une bicyclette/**
                                      un vélomoteur.

for one day/a week   **pour une journée/une semaine**

C **CAMPING.** Camping in France is a well-organized business, and while Breton sites may not figure among the most sophisticated in the country, they make up for it by remaining close to nature. Some sites offer incomparable views. Campsites are officially graded from one to four stars. The sites round Saint-Malo are often very full. For further information about camping consult the special leaflet issued by the French national tourist office.

"Camping sauvage", camping outside a site, is very widespread in certain areas—on Belle-Ile, for instance. If you camp on private property, ask the landowner for permission. You'll often come across signs *Camping à la ferme*, meaning that you can camp at the farm. *Camping interdit* means no camping.

Many British travel agencies/holiday companies offer caravanning or camping holidays in France, in caravans (trailers) or tents on sites, often including the cost of ferry crossings.

France-Inter, the radio station, provides up-to-date information regarding camping and camping sites; ring Paris 16 ~ (1) 43.06.13.13 between 8 a.m. and 9 p.m. during the week and between 8 a.m. and 4 p.m. on Saturdays.

Have you room for a tent/a   **Avez-vous de la place pour une**
caravan?   **tente/une caravane?**

May we camp on your land,   **Pouvons-nous camper sur votre**
please?   **terrain?**

CANAL TRIPS. There's no better way to see inland Brittany than by its network of navigable rivers and canals, making 375 miles in all. Numerous firms hire out boats of all kinds, from luxurious launches and *carabarges* (caravan-barges) to canoe-kayaks.

For further information contact: Comité national des Canaux bretons, 14, boulevard Beaumont, 35100 Rennes; or Comité de promotion touristique des Canaux bretons et voies navigables de l'Ouest, 3, rue des Portes-Mordelaises, 35000 Rennes. Alternatively take boat trips up the Odet, Aulne or Rance for some superb impressions.

CAR HIRE *(location de voitures)*. Car-hire firms throughout Brittany handle French-made cars and often foreign makes. Local firms sometimes offer lower prices than the big international companies.

To hire a car you must furnish a valid driving licence (held for at least one year) and your passport. Depending on the model you rent and the hiring firm, minimum age for renting a car varies from 21 to 25. Holders of major credit cards are normally exempt from advance deposit payments; otherwise you must pay a substantial (refundable) deposit for a car.

I'd like to hire a car tomorrow.	**Je voudrais louer une voiture pour demain.**
for one day/a week	**pour une journée/une semaine**

CHILDREN. Brittany has all the ingredients for successful family holidays. If it rains or you are looking for ways to entertain children, why not visit one of the aquariums at Saint-Malo, Dinard, Concarneau, Roscoff or Rothéneuf or Vannes? The crazy shapes of the sculpted rocks at Rothéneuf by Saint-Malo fascinate most children, as does the birdlife of Cap Sizun, the Sept-Iles (Perros-Guirec), Cap Fréhel and La Brière. As to zoos, there's one at Branféré and in Château de la Bourbansais—both in lovely settings. A visit to a lighthouse (Eckmühl, Cap Fréhel, Pointe Saint-Mathieu, etc.) gives an insight into the loneliness, responsibilities, and tribulations of a lighthouse-keeper's life. And naval museums (Brest, Camaret, Saint-Servan, etc.) provide an interesting background to seaside activity.

On the beach, there are clubs offering all kinds of sporting activities (see BABY-SITTING). Other activities you can join in yourself include minigolf; or leave children at any of the riding schools or sailing schools peppered along the coast—for an hour, a half day, a day or a week.

C **CLIMATE and CLOTHING.** Brittany's climate would be the envy of many a country: fig trees, mimosa, palm trees and hydrangea flourish. On Bréhat, Belle-Ile or in the Golfe du Morbihan, the vegetation is positively Mediterranean; even the winters are pleasantly supportable.

There is, of course, the rain—on average 190 days a year—but it comes and goes. Temperatures remain mild all year round.

Obviously, too, even in midsummer, it's sensible to go to Brittany prepared for less than a heat wave, if only because of the wind. Heavy Breton jerseys offer ideal protection against the wind and rain, and the *ciré* (weatherproof coat) often comes in handy. Rainboots and an anorak can be useful. (See also When to Go, p. 106.)

COMMUNICATIONS

Post office *(poste).* French post offices display a sign with a stylized blue bird and/or the words *Postes et Télécommunications* or *P & T.* In cities, the main post office is open from 8 a.m. to 7 p.m., Monday to Friday, and 8 a.m. to noon on Saturdays. In smaller towns the hours are usually from 8.30 a.m. to noon, and 2.30 to 5 or 6 p.m., Monday to Friday; 8 a.m. to noon on Saturdays.

In addition to normal mail service, you can make local or long-distance telephone calls, send telegrams and receive or send money at any post office.

Note: You can also buy stamps *(timbres)* at a tobacconists and, occasionally, at hotels and from postcard or souvenir vendors.

Poste restante (general delivery). If you don't know ahead of time where you'll be staying, you can have your mail addressed to you in any town c/o *Poste restante, Poste centrale.* You can collect it only on presentation of your passport. British visitors may have to ask staff to look under "E" for Esquire. A small fee is charged.

Telegrams. All local post offices accept domestic and overseas telegrams. You may also dictate a telegram over the telephone (dial 36.55).

Telephone *(téléphone).* Long-distance and international calls can be made from any phone box, but if you need assistance in placing the call, go to the post office or get your hotel to do it. If you want to make a reverse-charge (collect) call, ask for *un appel en PCV* (pronounced: pay-say-vay). For a personal (person-to-person) call, specify *un appel avec préavis pour* . . . (naming the party you want to talk to).

Phone boxes *(cabine téléphonique* or *taxiphone)* are scattered round the towns and countryside. There are two types of payphones. One takes a range of coins, the other is card operated. Telecards are sold at post offices, railway ticket counters and shops recognized by a "Télé-carte" sign, and are available for 40 or 120 charge units. If you make a call from your hotel, a café or a restaurant, you are likely to be charged a little extra.

C

To make an international call, dial 19 and wait until there is a continous burr tone. The international code numbers are posted in all phone boxes. For long-distance calls within France, there are no area codes (just dial the 8-digit number of the person you want to call), *except* when telephoning from Paris or the Paris region to the provinces (dial 16 and wait for the dialling tone, then dial the 8-digit number of the subscriber and from the provices to Paris or the Paris region (dial 16, wait for the dialling tone, then dial 1 followed by the 8-digit number). If you need the assistance of an operator, dial 36.10.

express (special delivery)	**exprès**
airmail	**par avion**
registered	**recommandé**
Have you any mail for ...?	**Avez-vous du courrier pour ...?**

CONSULATES and EMBASSIES. Contact your consulate or embassy when in trouble (loss of passport, theft or loss of all your money, problems with the police, serious accident). The United Kingdom maintains consulates in Nantes and Dinard. Citizens of other countries should get in touch with their representatives in Paris.

Australia (embassy and consulate): 4, rue Jean-Rey, 75015 Paris; tel. 16~(1) 45.75.62.00.

Canada (embassy-chancellery): 35, avenue Montaigne, 75008 Paris; tel. 16~(1) 47.23.01.01.

Eire (embassy-chancellery): 12, avenue Foch (enter from 4, rue Rude), 75016 Paris; tel. 16~(1) 45.00.20.87.

New Zealand (embassy-chancellery 7ter, rue Léonard-de-Vinci, 75116 Paris; tel. 16~(1) 45.00.24.11.

South Africa (embassy): 59, quai d'Orsay, 75007 Paris; tel. 16~(1) 45.55.92.37.

United Kingdom (consulate): 6, rue Lafayette, 44000 Nantes; tel. 40.48.57.47.
8, avenue de la Libération, 35800 Dinard; tel. 99.46.26.64.

U.S.A. (embassy-chancellery): 2, avenue Gabriel, 75382 Paris, Cedex 08; tel. 16~(1) 42.96.12.02.
(consulate): 2, rue St. Florentin, 75042 Paris, Cedex 01; tel. 16~(1) 42.96.12.02.

113

C **CRIME and THEFT.** Watch your wallet and handbag, especially in crowds. Keep items of value in your hotel safe and obtain a receipt for them. It's a good idea to leave large amounts of money there as well.

Lock your car at all times and leave nothing valuable inside, or put what you're leaving in the locked boot (trunk). The car parks at seaside lookout points (e.g. Pointe du Van) are classic targets for thieves. Any loss or theft should be reported at once to the nearest *commissariat de police* (see POLICE).

I want to report a theft.	**Je veux signaler un vol.**
My ticket/wallet/passport/ handbag/credit card has been stolen.	**On m'a volé mon billet/porte- feuille/passeport/sac à main/ (ma) carte de crédit.**

D **DRIVING IN FRANCE.** To take a car into France, you will need:

- A valid driving licence
- Car registration papers
- Insurance coverage (the green card is no longer obligatory but com- prehensive coverage is advisable)
- A red warning triangle and a set of spare bulbs

Drivers and front-seat passengers are required by law to wear seat belts. Children under 10 may not travel in the front (unless the car has no back seat). Driving on a provisional licence is not permitted in France. Minimum age is 18.

Driving regulations: Drive on the right, overtake on the left. (*Serrez à droite* means "keep to the right".) British drivers should be careful not to forget momentarily that they should be driving on the right, such as when they emerge from a one-way-street, a refuelling stop or at a T-junction. In built-up areas, give automatic priority to vehicles coming from the right. The priority will be taken in any case so it's only wise to "offer" it first. But the *priorité* rule does not apply at roundabouts (traffic circles). Outside built-up areas—at junctions marked by signs with a cross or a yellow square on a white back- ground—the more important of two roads has right of way.

French drivers have become less reckless of recent years and stricter law enforcement has meant considerably fewer virtuosos showing off. Refrain from drinking and driving: if you're stopped with over 0.8 milligrams in the blood, even if there's been no accident, there may be trouble ahead.

Speed limits: On dry roads, 130 kph (around 80 mph) on toll motor- ways (expressways), 110 kph (68 mph) on dual carriageways (divided ighways), 90 kph (56 mph) on all other roads, and 45 or 60 kph (28 or 37 mph) in built-up areas. *Note:* when roads are wet, all limits are reduced by 10 kph (6 mph). The word *rappel* means a restriction is continued.

Signposting, adequate on the main roads, can be maddeningly insufficient when it comes to finding castles, small *communes,* villages, or churches in the Breton countryside. The number of hamlets that begin with "Ker", "Pen" or "Lan" confuses the issue (see LANGUAGE). Note that *port de plaisance* means yacht harbour, *commissariat,* police station, *hôtel de ville* or *mairie,* town hall, and *grève* or *plage,* beach.

Road conditions: Generally speaking, roads in Brittany are good. Toll-free dual carriageways, mostly semi-completed, connect the main towns, forming a circuit round the province. There is still no easy way across the interior. Leisurely driving is a pleasure, hasty driving a nightmare, and virtually impossible anyway: roads twist, turn, mount and descend, taunting and tormenting motorists. Bridges over estuaries are few and far between, meaning long detours. Never underestimate distances.

Motorways/Expressways *(autoroute)* marked *à péage* charge tolls; the price varies but is usually quite high. You will find emergency telephones every two kilometres (about 1 mile) and 24-hour petrol stations every 20 kilometres (12 mi.).

France-Inter, the radio station, provides the latest information on road conditions: ring Paris 16 ~ (1) 48.58.33.33 24 hours a day.

Parking: In town centres, most street parking is metered. In blue zones (parking spaces marked with a blue line) you must display a *disque de stationnement* or parking clock (obtainable from petrol stations or stationers), which you set to show when you arrived and when you must leave. Some streets have alternate parking on either side of the street according to which half of the month it is (the dates are marked on the signs).

A quiet little country town or seaside resort with perfectly adequate off-season parking facilities turns into a chaotic free-for-all in the height of summer. Simply to cross Quimperlé or Saint-Jacut, let alone park there, can take an hour. The prudent try at crack of dawn, during lunch hour or late afternoon.

Breakdowns: It's wise to take out some form of internationally valid breakdown insurance before leaving home. Local garages provide towing and make on-the-spot repairs. Spare parts for European cars

D are readily available. Always ask for an estimate *before* undertaking repairs. TVA (VAT/sales tax) is added to the cost of repairs.

Fuel and oil *(essence; huile):* Fuel is available in super (98 octane), normal (90 octane), lead-free (95 octane) and diesel *(gas-oil)*. Service-station attendants expect a small tip.

Road signs: Most road signs are the standard international pictographs, but you may encounter these written signs as well:

Accotements non stabilisés	Soft shoulders
Chaussée déformée	Uneven road surface
Déviation	Diversion (detour)
Gravillons	Loose gravel
Péage	Toll
Priorité à droite	Yield to traffic from right
Ralentir	Slow down
Serrez à droite/à gauche	Keep right/left
Stationnement interdit	No parking

driving licence	**permis de conduire**
car registration papers	**carte grise**
Are we on the right road for ...?	**Sommes-nous sur la route de ...?**
Fill the tank, please.	**Le plein, s'il vous plaît.**
lead-free/normal/super	**sans plomb/normale/super**
I've had a breakdown.	**Ma voiture est en panne.**
There's been an accident.	**Il y a eu un accident.**

E **EMERGENCIES** *(urgence).* You can get assistance anywhere in France by dialling the number 17 for the police *(police secours);* 18 for the fire brigade *(pompiers),* who also turn out for medical emergencies.

Careful	**Attention**	Police	**Police**
Fire	**Au feu**	Stop, thief!	**Au voleur!**
Help	**Au secours**		

Can you help me?	**Pouvez-vous m'aider?**

ENTRY FORMALITIES and CUSTOMS *(douane).* Nationals of
116 EEC countries and Switzerland need only a valid passport to enter

France. Nationals of other countries should check with the French consulate to see if they need a visa.

The following chart shows some main items you may take into France and, when returning home, into your own country:

Into:	Cigarettes		Cigars		Tobacco	Spirits	Wine
France 1)	200	or	50	or	250 g.	1 l. and	2 l.
2)	300	or	75	or	400 g.	1½ l. and	5 l.
3)	400	or	100	or	500 g.	1 l. and	2 l.
Canada	200	and	50	and	900 g.	1.1 l. or 1.1 l.	
Eire 1)	200	or	50	or	250 g.	1 l. and	2 l.
2)	300	or	75	or	400 g.	1½ l. and	5 l.
U.K. 1)	200	or	50	or	250 g.	1 l. and	2 l.
2)	300	or	75	or	400 g.	1½ l. and	2 l.
U.S.A.	200	and	100	and	4)	1 l. or	1 l.

1) If arriving from EEC countries with duty-free items or from other European countries.
2) If arriving from EEC countries with non-duty free items.
3) Residents outside Europe.
4) A reasonable quantity.

British visitors may also bring back from France £120 worth of goods duty free.

There's no limit on the importation or exportation of local or foreign currencies or traveller's cheques, but amounts exceeding 50,000 French francs or equivalent must be declared on arrival.

I've nothing to declare.	**Je n'ai rien à déclarer.**
It's for my own use.	**C'est pour mon usage personnel.**

HOURS *(heures d'ouverture)*

Banks tend to open from 9 a.m. to noon and 2 to 4 p.m. on weekdays, and close either on Saturdays (main towns) or Mondays. All banks close on major national or regional holidays and most close early on the day preceding a public holiday.

H **Main post offices:** 8 a.m.–7 p.m. weekdays, 8 a.m.–noon Saturdays.

Groceries, bakeries, food shops: 7 a.m.–7 p.m. Monday–Saturday. Food shops are often open on Sunday mornings—bakeries, butchers, charcuteries, in particular, but also some supermarkets.

Other shops: 9 or 9.30 a.m.–6.30 or 7 p.m. Monday to Saturday. Many shops close all or half of Monday.

Museums, châteaux and **monuments:** 10 a.m. (variable)–5.30 p.m. Closing day is usually Tuesday. During low-season, many close or have reduced hours.

Food markets: Most towns have a fruit and vegetable market; enquire locally about the day. Fish markets are set up beside the port when the boats come in. The larger fishing towns such as Lorient and Concarneau have *criées* (fish auctions) at crack of dawn or late at night.

L **LANGUAGE.** Don't call Breton a dialect or patois—it's a language, and a living one at that, making a comeback after years of neglect. Its use is essentially confined to Finistère, Côtes-du-Nord and part of Morbihan; an invisible line runs from Saint-Brieuc across to Vannes, separating the Breton-speaking from the French- or Gallo-speaking (the local French patois) areas. In fact *everybody* speaks French.

Breton resembles Welsh and, to a lesser extent, Irish and Gaelic. Although Bretons can understand none of these, many words have the same origin and are close.

Bretons, like the French as a whole, speak foreign languages grudgingly, so if at all possible, struggle along in French. Never take an understanding of English for granted.

Here's a mini-glossary of common Breton words that are handy to know, many of which appear in place-names:

biniou = bagpipes	**lan** = religious community, hermitage
Breizh = Brittany	
bro = region	**loc** = monastery
coat/goat = wood	**men** = stone
coz = old	**mor** = sea
fest noz = (night-time) party	**pen** = head (point), cape
Itron = Virgin	**plou** = parish, village
kenavo = goodbye	**tre/trez** = village, hamlet
ker = house, village	**ty** = house

The Berlitz phrase book FRENCH FOR TRAVELLERS covers almost all situations you're likely to encounter in your travels in France. If further help is required, the Berlitz French-English/English-French pocket dictionary contains the basic vocabulary a tourist will need, plus a menu-reader supplement.

Goodbye	**Au revoir**
You're welcome.	**Je vous en prie.**
Speak slowly, please.	**Parlez lentement, s'il vous plaît.**
I didn't understand.	**Je n'ai pas compris.**

MEDICAL CARE and HEALTH. (See also EMERGENCIES.) Make sure your health insurance policy covers illness or accident while on holiday. If not, ask your insurance representative, automobile association or travel agent about special holiday insurance plans.

Visitors from EEC countries with corresponding health insurance facilities are entitled to medical and hospital treatment under the French social security system. Before leaving home, insure that you are eligible and have the appropriate forms (E111) required to obtain this benefit in case of need. Doctors who belong to the French social security system *(médecins conventionnés)* charge the minimum.

If you're taken ill or have a toothache, your hotel receptionist can probably recommend an English-speaking doctor or dentist; otherwise, ask at the *Syndicat d'Initiative,* or in an emergency the *gendarmerie.*

Chemists *(pharmacie)* display green crosses. Staff are helpful in dealing with minor ailments and can recommend a nurse *(infirmière)* if you need injections or other special care. The *gendarmerie* will give addresses of pharmacies open at night (on a rota system); the name and address of the nearest pharmacy on duty *(jour/semaine de garde)* is noted in the window of all other pharmacies.

A problem you might meet is over-exposure to the sun. Because of the sea breeze in Brittany, you may not realize just how much sun you're getting, leading to uncomfortable consequences.

Where's the chemist on duty?	**Où est la pharmacie de garde?**
I need a doctor/a dentist.	**Il me faut un médecin/un dentiste.**
an upset stomach/a fever/ sunburn	**mal à l'estomac/de la fièvre/ un coup de soleil**
I have a pain here.	**J'ai mal ici.**

MEETING PEOPLE. The Bretons are a strange people, contradictory, eccentric, superstitious and naive, yet wary and worldly-wise.

M Rooted in tradition yet imaginative, they uphold their Breton heritage with distinct pride. Profoundly French, generous, witty, garrulous, great story-tellers, they can also be vague, meditative, taciturn. The friendliness is genuine, but it's not as forthcoming as further south. The French as a whole are an expansive people and are frustrated when people do not communicate.

Celtic reunions—particularly the Lorient Festival—bring together all the Celtic peoples for folklore displays, and there are, despite historical vicissitudes, many characteristics in common.

Beach activities and team sports inevitably lead to contacts. And, of course, there are discos, cafés and the beach promenades. Wherever you find yourself, a simple *bonjour* (good day), a smile, a *s'il vous plaît* (please) or a *merci* (thanks) will go a long way.

French people kiss or shake hands when greeting each other or saying goodbye. When you're introduced to someone or meeting a friend you're expected to shake hands at least. Close friends are kissed on both cheeks.

MONEY MATTERS

Currency. The French *franc* (abbreviated F or FF) is divided into 100 *centimes* (ct.).

Coins: 5, 10, 20, 50 ct.; 1, 2, 5, 10 F.

Banknotes: 20, 50, 100, 200, 500 F.

For currency restrictions, see ENTRY FORMALITIES AND CUSTOMS.

Banks and currency exchange. (See also HOURS.) Local tourist offices *may* change money outside banking hours at the official bank rate. Take your passport along when you go to change money or traveller's cheques. Your hotel may also come to the rescue, though you'll get a less favourable rate of exchange. The same applies to foreign currency or traveller's cheques changed in stores, boutiques or restaurants.

Credit cards are being used in an increasing number of hotels, restaurants, shops, petrol stations, etc.

Traveller's cheques and **Eurocheques** are widely accepted throughout France. Outside the towns, it's preferable to have some ready cash with you.

Sales tax. Called TVA, a value added sales tax is imposed on almost all goods and services. In hotels and restaurants, this is accompanied by a service charge.

Visitors from non-EEC countries will be refunded the TVA on larger purchases. Ask the salesperson who serves you for the requisite form, to be filled out and handed to French customs on departure.

Where's the nearest bank/currency exchange office?	**Où se trouve la banque/le bureau de change la/le plus proche?**
I want to change some pounds/dollars.	**Je voudrais changer des livres sterling/des dollars.**
Do you accept traveller's cheques/this credit card?	**Acceptez-vous les chèques de voyage/cette carte de crédit?**

NEWSPAPERS and MAGAZINES *(journaux; magazines).* During the tourist season, you can be pretty certain—barring a strike at one end or the other—of getting major British and Continental newspapers and news magazines on publication day or the following morning. The Paris-based *International Herald Tribune* is certainly available at main news agents in resorts and larger towns. *Ouest-France* publishes regional newspapers with listings of all local events, so it's well worth keeping an eye on their "what's on locally" sections.

POLICE. In cities and larger towns, you'll see the blue-uniformed *police municipale;* they are the local police force who direct traffic, keep order and investigate crime.

Outside the main towns are the *gendarmes;* they wear blue trousers and black jackets with white belts and are also responsible for traffic and crime investigation. Contrary to the French opinion of their police force, foreigners usually find these representatives of law and order pleasant, helpful and (often) efficient; few know foreign languages, however.

The dreaded *C.R.S.,* the national security force, usually seen with helmets, truncheons and visors, are only called in to deal with emergencies and degenerating demonstrations. The equally threatening-looking *garde mobile,* called *"motards"* or *police de la route,* patrol the roads, often in pairs, on powerful bikes. Don't forget that an ignorance of French excuses nothing—least of all speeding offences.

Throughout Brittany, in case of need, dial 17 for police assistance.

PUBLIC HOLIDAYS *(jours fériés).* Following are the national French holidays. If one of these holidays falls just before or after a weekend, many Frenchmen prolong things (but this doesn't usually affect shops or businesses).

P

January 1	*Jour de l'An*	New Year's Day
May 1	*Fête du Travail*	Labour Day
May 8	*Fête de la Libération*	Victory Day
July 14	*Fête nationale*	Bastille Day
August 15	*Assomption*	Assumption
November 1	*Toussaint*	All Saints' Day
November 11	*Armistice*	Armistice Day (1918)
December 25	*Noël*	Christmas Day
Movable dates:	*Lundi de Pâques*	Easter Monday
	Ascension	Ascension
	Lundi de Pentecôte	Whit Monday

In France, school holidays are staggered by regions, but, as elsewhere, resorts tend to fill up in the holiday season. In general, children's summer holidays begin in late June and go on to mid-September. August can be appallingly crowded in big centres and on the more popular beaches.

Are you open tomorrow?   **Est-ce que vous ouvrez demain?**

T **THALASSOTHERAPY** *(thalassothérapie)*. The invigorating effects of iodine-rich sea air and sea water have been known for a long time, but it's only fairly recently that specific therapeutic treatments have been developed utilizing sea water, sea mud, algae, etc. Respiratory ailments, rheumatic complaints, arthritis, vein and muscle problems, obesity and nervous disorders can all be treated with thalassotherapy. Various centres (many linked to a hotel) have been established in Brittany: at Paramé, at Perros-Guirec, Roscoff, Tréboul-Douarnenez, Bénodet, Quiberon (first and most famous of the institutes), Carnac, Pornichet. For full information, write either to the local *Syndicat d'Initiative* or to:

Comité régional du Tourisme, 3, rue d'Espagne, 35022 Rennes; tel. 99.50.11.15.

TIME DIFFERENCES. France keeps to Central European Time (GMT + 1). Summer time (GMT + 2) comes into force from late March to end September. The days are long at the height of summer, when it's still light at 11 p.m. The following chart gives summer time **122** differences.

New York	London	**France**	Sydney	Auckland
6 a.m.	11 a.m.	**noon**	8 p.m.	10 p.m.

What time is it?   **Quelle heure est-il?**

TIPPING. A longlife fief of the automatic and regular tip, France is going through a change of mind. Nowadays, a 10 to 15% service charge is usually added directly to hotel and restaurant bills—but not always. Be on the lookout for the 10–15% extra and the words *service en sus* or *service non compris*.

Rounding off the overall bill helps round off friendship with waiters, too. Taxi drivers should get 10–15%, as should hairdressers and barbers. Filling station attendants and cinema ushers *definitely* expect a coin. See the chart below for a further thumb-nail guide.

Porter, per bag	4–5 F
Hotel maid, per week	20–40 F
Bellboy, errand	4–5 F
Lavatory attendant	2 F
Filling station attendant	2–3 F
Guide, half day	20–30 F
Cinema usher	2–3 F

TOILETS. Public facilities are not, as a rule, France's glory. Beaches tend to be undersupplied, and the cafés beside the beach promenade can scarcely claim to heights of hygiene. Stand-up facilities can be harrowing; the wash basin and towel are not always clean. Better hotels will have superior facilities, but they may not be round the corner.

Café facilities are generally free, but you should order at least a coffee if you use the toilet. If there is no light-switch, the light will usually go on when you lock the door. A saucer with small change on it means you are expected to leave a tip.

Women's toilets may be marked *Dames,* men's either *Messieurs* or *Hommes.*

Where are the toilets, please?   **Où sont les toilettes, s'il vous plaît?**

T **TOURIST INFORMATION OFFICES** *(Office du tourisme/Syndicat d'Initiative).* French national tourist offices abroad help with planning your holiday, with itineraries and suggestions, with brochures, timetables and maps and ideas for specific types of holiday (but they cannot make bookings for you).

Some addresses:

Canada	1981 McGill College Avenue, Suite 490, Esso Tower, Montreal, Que. H3A 2W9; tel. (514) 288-4264
	1 Dundas Street West, Suite 2405, P.O. Box 8, Toronto, Ont. M5G 1Z3; tel. (416) 593-4717
Great Britain	178, Piccadilly, London W1V 0AL; tel. (01) 493-6594
U.S.A.	645 N. Michigan Avenue, Suite 430, Chicago, IL 60611; tel. (312) 337-6301
	9401 Wilshire Boulevard, Room 840, Beverly Hills, CA 90212; tel. (213) 272-2661
	610 Fifth Avenue, New York, NY 10020; tel. (212) 757-1125
	1 Hallidie Plaza, San Francisco, CA 94102; tel. (415) 986-4174

In France, each town of any importance—and many small places as well, with specific sights of interest—have a *Syndicat d'Initiative* (a local tourist office) either indicated by the initials I, S.I. or the words *Office du tourisme,* mostly found near the centre of town at the station or at the port. Usually, particularly in small offices, the staff go to great pains to help. They are an absolute mine of information on local and regional possibilities, with lists and brochures, train, bus and ferry timetables, tables of high and low tides, suggestions of excursions, visits and activities, etc. They may not actually recommend restaurants, however—at least officially. Although hours vary, most offices are open from 9.30 a.m.–1 p.m. and 2–6.30 p.m. (off season, many are closed or work on greatly reduced hours) daily except Sunday. Most have English-speaking personnel, but any attempt to speak French will be appreciated.

TRANSPORT. Because of the configuration of the country and the fact that the coast makes it hard to follow a straight route, it's not always easy to get from one town to another, even if they're only a few miles apart. You may have to make considerable detours or wait for a few hours en route. A car, a bicycle—or even just a plain pair of shoes—are often the best means of getting around.

Buses. Bus tickets are purchased in the bus-stations. Many of Brittany's bus companies are run by the SNCF, or French National Railways system, that has replaced the less frequented rail routes by less onerous buses. Times are often made to fit in with the arrival of trains. Bus stations, however, are virtually always near the centres of towns or their railway stations.

Between major towns buses are speedy, efficient and not expensive, with a bit of local colour often included (free) and some agreeable sightseeing (on certain routes).

Coach tours to points of scenic or historic interest in specific regions are numerous. Look for advertisements in hotel lobbies, at tourist offices, railway and bus stations, who also give out timetables.

Island Boats and Ferries. Launch services *(vedettes),* often part of the French Railways (SNCF), operate between the islands (Belle-Ile, Bréhat, Ile aux Moines, etc.) and the mainland all year round (but with considerably reduced schedules outside the peak holiday season). Schedules are posted clearly at embarkation points, but you can always obtain your own from the local *Syndicat d'Initiative.* Times often depend on tides. In winter, programmes can be curtailed owing to weather conditions.

Air Services. A taxi plane runs regularly from Brest to Ouessant (20 mins.) at certain times of the year.

Taxis. Taxis are plentiful in Breton towns and *bourgs.* They are advertised under "Taxis" in the local telephone directory and noted in local tourist office literature. Vehicles are metered, but if your ride takes you out of town, you may have to pay for the return journey; check before starting. Cabs can be called by telephone; in towns of any size there will be one or two waiting at the station, or they can be called easily from there. By European standards, fares are reasonable, with rates usually higher in small towns where runs are shorter. There is always a supplement for baggage. Some taxis are not insured to take more than three passengers.

Trains. The SNCF *(Société Nationale des Chemins de Fer Français),* the national railways, operate fast, clean and comfortable trains from Paris-Montparnasse to Brest direct via Le Mans, Vitré, Rennes, Saint-Brieuc and Morlaix. Other major lines cover main towns—Nantes, Lorient, Quimper—but the coast and minor inland towns are either poorly served or not served at all. Coaches and buses take over from trains at many points or small local trains (*autorail* or *michelines*) link certain localities.

Don't forget to validate your ticket by inserting it in one of the orange upright machines called a *machine à composter* or *composteur*. If it is not clipped and dated, the conductor *(contrôleur)* is entitled to fine you on the train.

Various categories of tickets, such as *Billet Touristique, Billet de Groupe, Billet de Famille, France Vacances,* that provide reductions, are available for groups, families, etc. Enquire at the station. Old-age pensioners are elegible for the *Carte Vermeil,* that means considerable savings. Eurailpasses and Inter-Rail cards are valid throughout Europe. N.B. Certain categories of ticket (e.g. *France Vacances*) must be bought *before* reaching France. See also p. 105.

SOME USEFUL EXPRESSIONS

yes/no	**oui/non**
please/thank you	**s'il vous plaît/merci**
excuse me	**excusez-moi**
where/when/how	**où/quand/comment**
how long/how far	**combien de temps/à quelle distance**
yesterday/today/tomorrow	**hier/aujourd'hui/demain**
day/week/month/year	**jour/semaine/mois/année**
left/right	**gauche/droite**
good/bad	**bon/mauvais**
big/small	**grand/petit**
cheap/expensive	**bon marché/cher**
old/new	**vieux/neuf**
open/closed	**ouvert/fermé**
Does anyone here speak English?	**Y a-t-il quelqu'un ici qui parle anglais?**
I don't understand.	**Je ne comprends pas.**
Please write it down.	**Veuillez bien me l'écrire.**
Help me, please.	**Aidez-moi, s'il vous plaît.**
I'd like ...	**J'aimerais ...**
How much is that?	**C'est combien?**
Waiter/Waitress, please!	**S'il vous plaît!**

Index

An asterisk (*) next to a page number indicates a map reference. Where there is more than one set of page references, the one in bold type refers to the main entry. For index to Practical Information, see inside front cover.